G000039358

St John in Cornwall

Ex Libris

R. E. Channing

Sir Francis Drake

by the same author

*

CAPTAIN COOK
(*Faber and Faber*)

*

PACIFIC HORIZONS
(*Allen and Unwin*)

THE VOYAGES OF CAPTAIN COOK
(*ed. The Cresset Library*)

Sir Francis Drake

CHRISTOPHER
LLOYD

FABER AND FABER
London · Boston

First published in 1957
by Faber and Faber Limited
3 Queen Square London WC1N 3AU
First published in this edition in 1979
Printed in Great Britain by
Whitstable Litho Ltd Whitstable Kent
All rights reserved

© Charles Christopher Lloyd 1957, 1979

CONDITIONS OF SALE

This book is sold subject to the condition that it shall not, by way of
trade or otherwise, be lent, re-sold, hired out or otherwise circulated
without the publisher's prior consent in any form of binding or cover
other than that in which it is published and without a similar condition
including this condition being imposed on the subsequent purchaser

British Library Cataloguing in Publication Data

Lloyd, Christopher, b. 1906
    Sir Francis Drake.
    1. Drake, Sir Francis   2. Admirals – England
    – Biography   3. Explorers – England –
    Biography
    942.05'5'0924   DA86.22.D7

    ISBN 0–571–11444–X

Contents

Map

Sketch Map of the New World and the Pacific
to illustrate Drake's operations in the West Indies
and part of his voyage round the world

page 39

Preface

The career of Sir Francis Drake arouses perennial interest. In his own day men followed him 'for friendship's sake and the renown of his name'. During the next century the spell cast by his legendary successes on the Spanish Main inspired generations of buccaneers to follow where he had led, though their booty was never as great as his. Eighteenth-century circumnavigators recalled his 'famous voyage' as their model. In our own day some words which he wrote when engaged in 'singeing the King of Spain's beard' have been incorporated in a prayer which is in daily use. His house in Devonshire has become a Drake Museum, while his visit to California has resulted in the formation of a Drake Navigators Guild in San Francisco.

The object of a brief biography such as this is to present the story of a man who has become one of the legendary figures of history to a generation of new Elizabethans. It is not written in the spirit of hero-worship, because Drake's achievements are great enough to make an uncritical account of them impertinent as well as misleading. Not everything that he did was morally right, nor even successful. His life, it seems to me, rises like a comet over a horizon of obscure, semi-piratical adventures. Success on his own account brought recognition and respectability, first, in the guise of a privateer's commission for his voyage round the world, and later as what we should call a naval officer (the term would be incomprehensible to an Elizabethan) in command of expeditionary forces and fleets in the war against Spain. His career reaches its climacteric at the battle of Gravelines towards the end of the Armada campaign. After that, the story is one of failure and disgrace until his tragic death near the scene of his earliest and most successful adventures.

Every writer on the subject must acknowledge his debt to Sir Julian Corbett's standard biography, *Drake and the Tudor Navy*, published in 1898. Since that date, and especially within the last ten years, a great deal more has been discovered about Drake's career. A glance at the lists of books printed at the end of this volume will show how much we are indebted to the publications of the Hakluyt Society and the Navy Records Society in this respect, as well as to the work of such investigators as Dr. Williamson, Professor Taylor, Professor Wernham, Mr. H. R. Wagner and Miss Irene Wright. Indeed the chief justification for a book of this sort is to bring to the attention of readers who do not normally reach such learned publications the fruits of modern scholarship in this particular field. If such readers are encouraged thereby to read for themselves such stirring adventure stories as the original narratives—*Sir Francis Drake Revived*, for example, or *The World Encompassed*—so much the better.

Though we can no longer regard Drake simply as the Protestant Hero, or the Devon Sea Dog of drawing-room ballads, we can and should admire his real achievements. His buccaneering adventures are as exciting as *Treasure Island*; his circumnavigation of the globe is the monumental feat of Elizabethan seamanship; while the part he played in the war against Spain entitles him to be regarded as the first great admiral to achieve an international reputation.

CHAPTER ONE

*

The Man and His Age

Francis Drake, wrote a Spanish lawyer who met him at the age of forty-six, 'is a man of medium stature, fair, rather heavy than slender, merry, careful. He commands and governs imperiously. He is feared and obeyed by his men. He punishes resolutely. Sharp, restless, well spoken, inclined to generosity and to ambition, vainglorious, boastful, not very cruel. These are the qualities I noted in him during my negotiations with him.' Since the negotiations were concerned with the sack of a city on the Spanish Main, it is a fair testimonial from an enemy.

The portrait is amplified by an Englishman writing after the name of Drake had become synonymous with that of England: 'low of stature, of strong limbs, broad-breasted, round-headed, with brown hair, full-bearded, his eyes round, large and clear, well-favoured, fair, and of a cheerful countenance.' He was, admittedly, 'ambitious for honour, and greatly affected to popularity', qualities which, in the highly competitive society of Elizabethan England, rendered him open to criticism on the part of rivals of better birth than he was. Like Nelson, he was certainly not representative of what came to be called 'the silent service', nor did his love of braggadocio come amiss in that colourful epoch. A naval friend of later years agreed 'that he would speak much and arrogantly', and that such qualities rendered him unfit for supreme command; but, he continues, it was unjust to criticize him for his low birth and lack of education, because his record as a great captain ought to be enough to silence such envious voices.

Drake's origin was indeed so humble that we do not know when he was born: it may have been any time between 1540 and 1545. Like Shakespeare, he came of yeoman stock. His father, Edmund Drake, seems to have had some experience at sea before settling down as a farmer at Crowndale, near Tavistock, where Francis, one of twelve children, was born. Edmund's strong Protestant convictions resulted in his being driven out of the county of Devon by a Catholic mob in 1549. When Francis was a child the family was living in an old hulk at Gillingham in Kent, where his father was 'preacher' to the men working in what was to become Chatham Dockyard. Later he became vicar of the small Medway town of Upchurch.

It is clear that from his earliest years Francis inherited a detestation of Catholics: his father had been driven off his farm by them; his boyhood was passed in the period of the Marian persecutions; highly coloured stories of the cruelties of the Spanish Inquisition were current among the seafaring folk with whom he grew up; and the empire of Spain, blessed by the Pope as the instrument of the Counter-Reformation, threatened all that he held dear, as well as offering temptations of wealth appealing to every Devon seaman. A long tradition of piracy dating well beyond the days of Chaucer's shipman of Dartmouth, combined with a strong Protestant faith, moulded Drake into the champion of Elizabethan England. In his own person he embodied the twin causes of that war with Spain in which British sea power was born.

A valuable connection with a richer class was his relationship to the Hawkins family of Plymouth. It was the prosperity of this family which displaced Dartmouth as the chief

West-country port, and it was natural that as soon as Francis had served his apprenticeship in Thames coastal craft he should hitch his star to that of his prosperous uncle, William Hawkins, who was engaged in the African trade. William's son John, a few years older than his cousin Francis Drake, extended this trade to the business of transporting slaves from the Gulf of Guinea to the Spanish colonies in the Caribbean. He was the first Englishman to follow the example of the Portuguese in this infamous traffic on which the prosperity of the western ports came in time to depend, but it must be remembered that in those days slavery was regarded as a natural fact. If a European fell into the hands of a Turk, or an Algerine corsair from the Barbary Coast, he was enslaved; criminals served as slaves in the galleys of France and Spain; and negroes, of course, were regarded as made by nature to be the slaves of white men.

In November 1566, therefore, we find Francis Drake at Plymouth ready to join the third slaving voyage of John Hawkins, who had already assembled four ships there. These voyages were of a somewhat ambiguous character, because it was not yet certain whether Hawkins should be regarded as a peaceful trader (as he himself intended), or as an interloper whose activities bordered on those of a corsair (as was the official Spanish view). Such opposing attitudes involved matters of high policy, so that at the last moment Hawkins found himself involved in political complications in London. Hence it was under the command of Captain John Lovell that Drake first crossed the Atlantic. The part played by a twenty-four year old seaman whom nobody had ever heard of is necessarily obscure. The only thing we know about Drake on this voyage is that he converted a Welsh Catholic to Protestantism during its course, a fact which emerged from the latter's confession to the Inquisition some years later. It seems a curious way to have spent what must have been exciting days crossing the western ocean for the first time, but it is typical of Drake's strong religious feelings. The voyage itself passed off fairly satisfactorily, inasmuch as the slaves were landed at places on the Spanish Main such as Rio de la Hacha; but it seems doubtful if Lovell was paid for them. Twelve months later Hawkins was to complain to the governor of the place that Lovell had been tricked, while the governor for his part pretended that he had accepted the slaves under duress.

At any rate Lovell and Drake returned home safely in September 1567. A month later the latter sailed again on what Hakluyt calls 'the third troublesome voyage of Master John Hawkins', a voyage of epoch-making consequences not only to a young man in his middle twenties, but to the history of the nation.

II

Before we follow him to sea it will be as well to set the stage on which he was to act. There is no greater mistake in reading the lives of those 'strange Elizabethans' (as a modern writer has called them), than to imagine that their world was nearer to ours than it was to the medieval world out of which they had not yet fully evolved. The international position of England was not yet important. Society was still semi-feudal in character. It is often difficult for us to understand the way people thought and acted, so alien were their ways to ours. In particular, in everything pertaining to the sea—the build of their ships, the way they navigated them, their knowledge of a world still half explored—everything was totally different.

The first ten years of Elizabeth's reign was an undistinguished decade giving little promise of the great age which was to come. The Queen's unerring political instinct warned her to keep quiet, to let the country settle down after the religious upheavals of the past fifty years and to maintain friendly relations with foreign powers, since she possessed no regular army and only a few unseaworthy ships dating back to her father's day. Since Drake made his name as the champion of England against European Catholicism, and since it was his voyage round the world which put England on the map as a maritime power, we have to bear in mind that when he first went to sea England was a small, unknown country on the outskirts of the civilized world, compared with the great empire of Spain. The national awakening in maritime enterprise, in which he took the leading part, as well as the magnificent flowering of the national genius in the Elizabethan drama which marks the last decade of the century, were still unimaginably in the future. Before either the age of Drake or the age of Shakespeare dawned there was a period of inactivity as far as the chief glories which we connect with the Elizabethan age were concerned.

Compared with the states bordering the Mediterranean, or with those now called Belgium and Holland, England was a remote and backward island in Drake's boyhood. There had been a brief moment about the beginning of the century when it looked as if the country would be illumined by the rays of the Renaissance, whether from Italy or Flanders. The three voyages of John Cabot and his son Sebastian resulted in a claim to North America, but it was left to Jacques Cartier to follow up their work by founding New France on the other side of the Atlantic. Sebastian Cabot himself left this country for Spain about the time when Henry VIII ceased to be the model Renaissance prince in order to become a religious tyrant. There was no scope for an explorer like Cabot in Reformation England, so he did not return to London until the reign of Edward VI, when as an old man he inspired the first of the new voyages, that of Willoughby and Chancellor in search of a north-eastern route to Cathay, which resulted in the foundation of the Muscovy Company. But even that voyage of 1553 was not followed up until the Hawkins family began their oceanic voyages to the west coast of Africa and men began to think that a north-western route to Cathay and the Spice Islands offered more opportunities to a northern nation still anxious to avoid the political entanglements which would result from an infringement of the Spanish and Portuguese monopoly of the tropical world.

It was the religious revolution precipitated by the Reformation which was responsible for thus postponing overseas enterprise to a time when the country was not so bitterly rent by persecutions in the name of either the Protestant or the Catholic faiths. Drake's boyhood spans those troubled times, which left an imprint on his mind as ineradicable as it was in the minds of millions of others who lived through the bloody conflicts which divided Europe between northern Protestantism and southern Catholicism. During his career the issue was still in doubt in the Low Countries, where the Dutch rebels became Elizabeth's allies while Flanders remained the Spanish Netherlands, and in France where the Wars of Religion (later to be repeated on a still more disastrous scale in the Thirty Years' War in Germany) divided the country and invited foreign intervention. Just as in our own day, there was a conflict of faiths upheld by each side with uncritical fanaticism. One side of Drake's character was certainly that of the Protestant crusader. We have only to read the language used in his letters, or even in his official despatches to the government, to see that he was convinced he was doing the Lord's work. The hand of the Lord seemed to him to be discernible in everything which he did. Not for nothing was he the friend of John Foxe, whose *Book of Martyrs* retelling the stories of the Marian persecution remained for generations of popular reading second only in holiness to the Bible itself.

A geographical revolution occurred at the same time as the religious revolution. By the date Martin Luther appeared the great Spanish and Portuguese explorers had opened up the ocean routes for trade and colonization on the part of their respective nations. Columbus had discovered America, leaving a new world to be developed by an ungrateful country during the succeeding century. Vasco de Gama had led the ships of the West to make contact for the first time with the ancient civilizations of the East. Magellan's *Victoria* had encircled the globe itself. By the time Drake repeated that voyage sixty years later, the Spaniards were established in the Philippines, in addition to central and southern America, while the Portuguese had their 'factories' in the Spice Islands and southern China, as well as in Brazil.

As is well known, the world was divided between them by the Treaty of Tordesillas in 1494, which laid down that no unauthorized person could 'go for the sake of trade, or any other reason whatsoever, to the said countries after they have been discovered'. When, in 1580, Philip II became King of Portugal as well as King of Spain, the Spanish empire was more far-flung than even the British empire of a later date. Well might he write from the Escurial—that huge palace and monastery combined built on the bleakest plateau in Spain—of 'this bare mountain side, whence I rule the affairs of half the world'.

The English never officially admitted the line of demarcation along longitude 47° W. 'No peace beyond the line' was already the motto of French freebooters, or corsairs (as the Spanish called them) in the Caribbean, whither they were shortly to be followed by the man whom the Spanish Ambassador once called the 'master thief of the unknown (i.e. new) world'. It was, however, deemed wiser to explore possible alternative routes, north-east or north-west, to the Far East, especially as such routes offered better markets for English cloth than tropical countries. The Hawkins family of Plymouth, to whose fortunes Drake attached himself, preferred the West African trade, thereby involving themselves in difficulties with the Portuguese, which John Hawkins added to when he tried to sell African slaves to Spanish colonists on the other side of the Atlantic.

John Hawkins was, indeed, no pirate or freebooter. Nevertheless in Spanish eyes he was an interloper in forbidden seas. With the appearance of a man of the character and traditions of Francis Drake, such peaceful objectives as Hawkins evidently had in mind no longer became possible. War was inevitable, not only because of the gathering strength of expansionist tendencies in Elizabethan England, but also because Drake was the man he was—ambitious, pugnacious, resentful of Spanish claims and full of hatred for Catholic practices. In fact, his personal aims and convictions epitomized those of the nation at large.

Maritime expansion would have been impossible had it not been for important developments in shipbuilding about the turn of the century. At that time the seafaring nations of the Mediterranean were developing the caravel type of vessel (in which Columbus discovered America) into the larger sea-going galleon. From this the Portuguese later developed an even larger type of ship for their long voyages across the Indian Ocean, the carrack, a prototype of the great East Indiamen of the next century: the greatest prize Drake ever took was one such carrack returning fully laden from the Spice Islands.

But the galleon was the normal ocean-going vessel of the

sixteenth century. The name was very vague in its connotation when Henry VIII, the father of the British Navy, introduced such ships which he called indiscriminately 'galleons', 'galleasses' and 'great ships'—though the true galleasse as used by the Spanish in the Armada campaign was a cross between the old-style fighting galley propelled by oars, and the new type of warship, the sailing galleon. When Drake went to sea there were still a few of Henry's ships in service, but his early experience of one of them led him to favour a newer and more specifically English type of galleon of which the *Revenge*, built in 1575, was his favourite and his flagship in 1588. The older type was too clumsy to manœuvre with ease, and manœuvrability was everything when it was necessary to alter the course of a ship in order to bring a full broadside to bear. Such 'high-charged' ships, as they were called, with their towering poops, heavy forecastles projecting over the bows, and excessive weight of cannon which strained their timbers, were well enough adapted to repel boarders, but they were too unseaworthy, they offered too much wind resistance to make them manageable. As we shall see, many of these thousand-ton ships, such as the *Elizabeth Jonas*, *Triumph* and *White Bear*, remained in service at the time of the Armada; but the future lay with the smaller 'race built' galleon, such as the *Revenge* and *Golden Hind*, lying low in the water and carrying more of a beakhead than the old overhanging forecastle structure.

We know that the *Revenge* was ninety-two feet long, thirty-two feet in the beam, of about four hundred and fifty tons burden and mounted thirty-four guns broadside, though more could be carried on deck if desired. The smaller *Golden Hind*, of about one hundred tons, carried fourteen guns broadside and four more on her upper deck, but beyond a crude drawing of the latter ship we have little detailed knowledge of either of these famous vessels. Since there are no contemporary scale-models, few draughts and somewhat inaccurate pictures of Tudor ships, it is difficult to identify or describe a particular ship, most galleons carried four masts—foremast, mainmast, mizen and bonaventure mizen. They were square rigged on the first two masts, lateen (or triangular) rigged on the after two. All ships were multi-decked, so that one cannot speak of a main or gun deck, as in later line-of-battleships. Nor was there any distinction at that date between the merchant ship and the warship: each was heavily armed (since the seas swarmed with pirates), and each played an equal part in the sort of fleets Drake commanded. In such ships a sailor going forward from the lantern on the poop would descend to the half-deck, on which was the whipstaff to work the tiller, since the steering wheel had not yet been invented, and thence to the quarter-deck. At the mainmast he would go down a ladder into the waist, then up again to the fo'c'sle, where most of the crew had their quarters, and where the ship's bell was hung; then down again on to the beakhead projecting only a few feet above the water.

It was in the carving of the beakhead and figurehead that the Elizabethan taste for 'bravery', or ostentatious ornament as we should call it, could best be indulged. Nor must we forget the bright colours with which the hulls of these ships were painted: green and white, red and white, yellow or blue; or their love of flying streaming pennants and gaily coloured standards emblazoned with coats of arms which were often embroidered on the sails themselves. They did not, however, follow the Spanish custom of emblazoning their sails with religious symbols or images.

The main armament was mounted on the first covered deck, with a few heavier guns on a lower deck, or projecting below the stern galleries in which officers took their ease. Sussex guns were the cheapest in Europe, though bronze guns were more accurate and the science of gunnery was largely of Italian origin. The guns Drake chiefly used were not cannon or even demi-cannon, since these were so heavy they were apt to start the timbers of a ship, but culverins and demi-culverins firing a 17 lb. or 9 lb. solid iron shot, sometimes chained together to form chain-shot in order to dismast an enemy. There was also a murderous variety of small guns called perriers, falconets, sakers, serpentines and similar forgotten names. Bows and arrows, swords and pikes were still the favourite deck weapons, though arquebuses, the predecessor of the musket, were generally used by the soldiers carried on board.

Drake's career was typical of that of most professional seamen in that he started life as an adventurer acting entirely on his own account, after he had gained some experience on board a ship belonging to some relation, until he became a respectable privateer sailing with the Queen's commission or letter of marque, though still acting in a semi-private capacity. Only when war broke out (a point not easily decided in an age when war was seldom formally declared) did he become what we should call a naval officer in command of a royal ship paid by the Crown. Just as there was no distinction between the merchant ship and the warship, so there was no distinction between the captain of the one or the other: everything depended on who paid them. Thus, of the ships engaged in the Armada campaign only sixteen were owned by the Queen, the remaining fifty-three being hired by the Crown for the crisis.

What usually happened in wartime was that a privately owned ship was hired, together with her standing officers of whom the Master and the Boatswain were the most important, followed by the Gunner, Carpenter, Sailmaker,

Cook, Trumpeter and all those who made the ship go. The government then commissioned a Captain to command the ship (he might be a gentleman like Sir Walter Raleigh, or a seaman born and bred like Drake), who was assisted by another 'gentleman' officer, the Lieutenant. At that date the Lieutenant seems to have been chiefly employed in the more administrative or political aspects of the voyage rather than in running the ship. Just as the Lieutenant was not comparable with the modern officer of that rank in that he carried out the sort of duties one associates with a senior supply officer today, so the Elizabethan Midshipman was a tough petty officer responsible for repelling boarders amidships and not the junior officer which he became a hundred years later. The commander-in-chief of a squadron was called 'the General' and his flagship was usually, but not invariably, called 'the Admiral'. The Lord Admiral (still only very occasionally called Lord High Admiral) was primarily a great officer of state who seldom went to sea, though he was nominally responsible for the general direction of the Navy. The manning, maintenance and victualling of the Navy were, however, outside his province, being the responsibility of the Navy Board, of which John Hawkins became Treasurer after his first voyage with Drake. Throughout the latter's career there are indeed signs of a certain impatience with the more formal and administrative characters who were called the Principal Officers—the Treasurer, Surveyor, Comptroller and Clerk of the Ships. By contrast, the Lord Admiral's function was essentially executive and the office had been for the past two generations the preserve of the Howard family. Thus in the Armada campaign Lord Howard of Effingham as Lord Admiral commanded the fleet which Hawkins had virtually created and Drake really fought.

Since neither the hierarchy nor the traditions of the naval service were as yet established, one of the chief problems

Drake had to solve was that of command. Up till his day the old custom of settling affairs by a council of war had been the rule. What he insisted on was that one man alone should command a ship and bear all the responsibility, though he might take advice from other officers. This new conception of leadership (which we now take for granted) involved him in some of the most difficult incidents in his career.

Such were the officers—either gentlemen or seamen, seldom a combination of the two because the technical skill of a professional seaman and the way he was trained were despised in an aristocratic society. The sailors themselves were called 'mariners', either volunteering with enthusiasm for the sort of privateering raid in which Drake excelled, or being 'taken up', that is to say conscripted, when a great armament was fitting out. They were supplemented by soldiers who manned the guns and fired their arquebuses while the seamen set the sails. We know little about them as individuals, but a wise captain did well to follow Hawkins's advice if he wished to have a happy ship: 'Serve God daily; love one another; preserve your victuals; beware of fire, and keep good company.'

By the last injunction he meant that ships should keep together, and it is interesting to see how closely Drake follows his example in the instructions he left for his last voyage on which he shared the command with him. These open with an order to observe divine service on board twice a day and then go on to state that 'great care must be taken to keep company and to come to speak with your admiral twice a day'. Various signals to be observed follow. At night 'you shall keep no light in any of the ships, but only the light in the binnacle (where the compass was housed), and this with the greatest care it be not seen, excepting the admiral's ship; and to avoid the danger of fire, you must not bear about any candle or light in the ship, unless in a lantern'. Then comes an injunction which occurs in most of such instructions as have survived—'You must not permit any gambling in the ship, with cards or dice, by reason of the numerous quarrels usually resulting from that practice.' Drake, who was apt to swear somewhat himself, significantly omits the warning against 'detestable swearing, filthy tales or ungodly talk' which we find in the instructions delivered to Chancellor on an earlier voyage, though we may be sure that such a religious-minded man would punish anything savouring of blasphemy very severely. He concludes with a wise warning in a matter of life and death: 'You must take the greatest care to save the provisions.'

Since Drake insisted that a captain possessed unchallenged authority on board, he was capable of having a mutinous 'gentleman' officer put to death, as he did on his voyage round the world; and since there was no official disciplinary code, an Elizabethan captain could interpret the customary rules much as he liked. Such punishments were severe because, as Drake himself complained, sailors were 'the most envious people of the world and unruly without government'. An ordinary seaman found guilty of murder might be tied to the corpse and thrown overboard; if he drew a knife on an officer he would have his hand cut off; if he struck a shipmate and drew blood he could be ducked thrice at the yard-arm; if he stole, his head might be shaved and anointed with a mixture of feathers and boiling oil; if he fell asleep on watch, or was guilty 'of beastly or filthy talk at his mess, or did swear and blaspheme at cards or dice' he was beaten or towed ashore. Drake had the reputation of being a strict disciplinarian, so no doubt such punishments were in use on board the ships he commanded; but for the most part (as a Spanish witness testified) his men 'adored him'.

III

Our admiration for the seamen of that great age, and particularly for the first captain to take his ship round the world, is enhanced if we realize that they lacked three things which a modern sailor takes for granted—accurate charts, reliable means of navigation, and victuals that would keep. The three were intimately connected.

According to John Davis of Dartmouth, who wrote one of the earliest manuals of navigation, 'the sea compass, chart and cross staff are instruments sufficient for the seaman's use'. The Elizabethan compass was a 32-point card with a needle attached which was magnetized by rubbing it on a lodestone. Drake's precious stone about an inch long, mounted in silver, is still preserved at the National Maritime Museum at Greenwich, where there is also an intricate navigation instrument called Drake's Dial. It is too small to be of much practical use, but it is a beautiful piece of workmanship composed of seven parts including a compass, a tide table, a perpetual calendar for reckoning saints' days, a sundial and an astrolabe, the predecessor of the sextant and cross staff. The purpose of the last named was to take a sight of the sun at noon in order to determine the latitude. For some fifty years it had been possible to find out how far north or south you were, but to determine the longitude, complains a contemporary writer, 'is too tedious for seamen, since it requireth the deep knowledge of astronomy'. He recommends the seaman to keep an account of the way of his ship by the use of the log line—a piece of wood attached to a line marked off at intervals by knots of ribbon which was hove overboard while an officer stood by with a sand-glass in his hand to note the speed at which the knots were paid out, thereby deducing the speed at which his ship was passing through the water. From this he reckoned the distance travelled since the 'log' was last written up on a slate. Such a clumsy method of discovering how far east or west you were of the prime meridian (at that date running through the Azores) obviously led to gross errors. The reason why South America is shown so broad on the map illustrated facing page 33 is because, until the days of Captain Cook, no one could tell the true longitudes involved.

When such errors, often amounting to hundreds of miles, were transferred to maps, the consequences might be disastrous. Drake could not know if the Pacific was 3,000 or 5,000 miles wide; he could not therefore lay in a suitable amount of stores. If he did not die of thirst or starvation by underestimating the distance, he might die of scurvy as a result of the deficiencies of his diet: the disaster of his Lisbon expedition in 1589 was largely due to bad victualling. To judge from a voyage undertaken soon after his circumnavigation, the supplies on board the *Golden Hind* included biscuit, flour, dried peas, pickled pork, cheese, with sack (a type of sherry) or malmsey (madeira) to drink when the water went foul in the casks, as it always did after a few weeks—and the ship was sixty-eight days crossing the Pacific.

Two sorts of chart may be distinguished at that time—the large-scale inaccurate maps produced by geographers like Abraham Ortelius (whose atlas Drake used), whose partner was Gerard Mercator, and the small-scale manuscript charts known as 'portolans' which, within their limited areas, were astonishingly accurate. But those areas were chiefly the coasts of Europe—all others being the carefully guarded secrets of the best cartographers of the time, the Spanish and the Portuguese. In parts of the world unknown to Englishmen Drake solved his navigational difficulties by shanghaiing a Portuguese pilot and stealing a book of charts of the

Pacific off a prize. We know that on his longest voyage he carried three books on navigation—probably Eden's *Art of Navigation*, Bourne's *Regiment for the Sea* and Cunningham's *Cosmographical Glass* (all adapted from foreign works); but we may guess that from the days of his apprenticeship in coastal craft—the best possible training for a circumnavigator, as the career of Cook was to prove—he was the sort of practical navigator who sailed by Dead Reckoning, i.e. by lead, log and compass, rather than by the newfangled astronomical methods being introduced by mathematicians. He certainly sailed the seas with such uncanny success that he earned the reputation of being the greatest seaman of his age. It was as a tribute to this aspect of his genius that the first printed book of charts to be published in England, the *Mariner's Mirror*, was dedicated to him in 1588, the year in which England's naval power first impressed itself upon the world.

The English, wrote the best informed of foreign ambassadors, 'enjoy the reputation of being, above all western nations, expert and active in all naval operations, and great sea dogs'. It was men like Davis and Frobisher, Hawkins and Cavendish, who gave the country that reputation, but Drake's genius towers above them all. In an age when every courtier and merchant was willing to invest in a syndicate to finance a venture to the north-east, the north-west, the tropical shores of Africa, the new-found-land of America, or the various routes in search of the eastern spice trade, the sea captain who could get a good ship was the man prized above all others. The connection between such resolute seamen, the enterprising merchants who wished to expand their trade by subsidising voyages of exploration, and the courtiers who gambled by investing money in such projects, is of the utmost importance to an understanding of the maritime enterprises of the Elizabethan Age. Almost every voyage was subsidized by some such syndicate, and even acts of war like Drake's Descent on the Indies or his Lisbon expedition, were financed more by private venturers than by the government. William Sanderson, the west-country cloth merchant who financed so many of these projects, was so enamoured of such seamen that he named his three sons Raleigh, Drake and Cavendish: one is glad to know that his own name was perpetuated by John Davis of Dartmouth on one of his voyages in search of the North-West Passage, when an icy cape on the coast of Baffin Land was called Sanderson His Hope. Raleigh, like Grenville, Hatton or even Mr. Secretary Walsingham, exemplified rather the courtier who risked his money (and sometimes his life) in furthering such projects; it was men like Drake, Davis, Cavendish and Frobisher who provided the element of professional seamanship. Many such voyages proved disastrous; others barely paid for the cost of fitting them out; but if the venture was led by Drake it was almost sure to succeed, or to be 'made', as the saying was.

The epic of the scores of these Elizabethan voyages was written by Richard Hakluyt in his *Principall Navigations Voyages and Discoveries of the English Nation* which was published the year after the Armada. The vision of Britain's maritime destiny as a commonwealth 'founded upon the seas' was never more grandly expressed than in the Epistle Dedicatory, where, after saluting the progress made by his countrymen in their ventures overseas, he recalls as the climax of his story of maritime enterprise the famous circumnavigation of Sir Francis Drake, which established England's reputation as a seafaring nation:

'What English ships did heretofore anchor in the mighty river of Plate? Pass and repass the unpassable (in former opinion) strait of Magellan, range along the coast of Chili, Peru, and all the back side of Nova Hispania, further than any Christian ever passed, traverse the mighty breadth of the South Sea, land upon the Luzones in despight of the enemy, enter into alliance, amity and traffic with the princes of the Moluccas and the isle of Java, double the famous Cape of Bona Speranza, arrive at the island of Santa Helena, and last of all return home most richly laden with the commodities of China, as the subjects of this now most flourishing monarchy have done?'

CHAPTER TWO

★

The Disaster at San Juan De Ulua

On 2nd October, 1567, John Hawkins sailed from Plymouth in command of four hundred men on board two 'great ships' lent by the Queen—the *Jesus of Lubeck* of 700 tons and the *Minion* of 300—together with a few small ships, among which was the *Judith* of 50 tons, of which Francis Drake became master and commander in the course of the voyage.

It was not a military but a slave-trading expedition for which the old 700-ton *Jesus* was thought suitable. As her name implies, she had been bought into the Navy from the Hanseatic League by Henry VIII fifty years earlier. Even ten years before Hawkins sailed in her she was described as 'not worth repair'. No wonder she caused trouble from the start. Her high stern works made her unmanageable in the gale which they encountered soon after leaving port. Before the end of the voyage her timbers were so strained and the leaks in her hull so dangerous that she nearly foundered under her crew. Nevertheless she served her purpose in history. Because of this unhappy experience in a ship of the old type, both Hawkins and Drake were encouraged to build the new type of 'race built' galleon.

Having with some difficulty collected five hundred slaves on the Guinea coast, Hawkins proceeded to try to sell them as before at places on the Spanish Main. His position throughout the voyage continued to be ambiguous. He knew that the King of Spain had forbidden trading in those parts, yet he claimed that he sailed as a representative of the Queen of England, whose flag he flew. He asked politely for trading facilities, yet he threatened that if these were not granted he would take them by force. He even tried to bribe the authorities with offers to use his own force against French raiders if they would comply with his requests.

At first his demands were politely refused. But as he knew that the colonists wished to purchase the slaves and other cargo which he had to sell, he tried using a show of force to give the authorities an excuse to act as their subjects really wanted. The policy looked like succeeding until they reached Rio de la Hacha, where Drake and Lovell had been tricked a year before.

Drake was the first to arrive before the town in the *Judith*. He asked to be allowed to land in order to fill his water casks. The reply came in the form of ranging shots from the batteries before the town. Drake opened fire with better effect, and then withdrew out of range to await the arrival of the rest of the squadron.

As soon as Hawkins arrived he sent on shore a formal request to trade, together with a complaint of the treatment of Lovell on the last voyage. The governor answered that if he dared to land he would be fired on. Next day, therefore, Hawkins put ashore a landing party at a point two miles outside the town. A sharp encounter with enemy arque-busiers followed until resistance was quelled. Hawkins proceeded to sell eighty negroes to the governor at a price of five thousand gold *pesos*, and a hundred and fifty more to the colonists, who had shown little sympathy with their governor's attitude throughout the affair.

Trade was easier along the coast, though it was not thought advisable to try the same tactics with the governor of Cartagena, a much larger town. Having got rid of most of his cargo in this unsatisfactory way, Hawkins began to think of returning home by the usual route through the Florida channel.

Here they were in danger of being overtaken by the hurricane season. The flagship was by now in such an unseaworthy condition that it is incredible she was still afloat. One of those on board describes how the planks in her stern 'did open and shut with every sea . . . the leaks being as big as the thickness of a man's arm, so that the living fish did swim upon the ballast as in the sea'. If he lost one of the Queen's ships, however rotten an old hulk, Hawkins and his syndicate would have to pay for it, but to continue home in her in such a condition was madness. There was nothing for it but to seek refuge in the nearest harbour where they could patch her up. This was at San Juan de Ulua, the port of Vera Cruz.

All would have been well had it not been for the fact that, unknown to Hawkins, the new Viceroy of the Indies, Don Martin Enriquez, was expected at any moment with the annual treasure fleet from Seville. It is difficult to say who was the more embarrassed—the governor of San Juan, who saw his anchorage invaded by forbidden 'lutherans', or Hawkins, who realized that a hostile fleet greatly superior in number might make its appearance at any time before they had finished repairing their ships. He had no choice but to occupy an island in the bay and get to work as quickly as possible. Guns were landed and the ships hauled up on the beach ready for careening.

The very next day thirteen galleons of the treasure fleet— eleven merchantmen escorted by two warships—appeared at the entrance of the harbour. Don Martin found the port occupied by those very enemies of the Crown whom he had been sent out to extirpate. Hawkins was in no position to deny him entry to his own harbour, so negotiations were begun and hostages exchanged. Spanish records make it plain that the Viceroy never had any intention of keeping his promise to allow the English to depart freely once they had repaired their ships.

The ships of both squadrons were now drawn up on the shingle, their sterns anchored in deeper water to prevent them from swinging with the tide. The island was so small —hardly three hundred yards long—that there can have been little space between the rival ships and everything that was done in one camp must have been seen by the other. It soon became obvious to Hawkins that something was afoot. He sent Barrett, the master of the *Jesus*, to protest at what were evidently hostile preparations, while he himself sat down to a hurried supper. As he did so one of his companions seized the arm of the Spanish hostage who was already sitting at the table and drew a dagger from the latter's sleeve. For his part, Barrett was seized as soon as he came over the side of the Spanish flagship and thrust below hatches.

A trumpet sounded the signal for attack and a party of forty Spaniards lying concealed in a hulk alongside sprang up to attack the English flagship. English guns opened fire and rival parties on shore began to attack each other. For two hours a confused fight at close quarters continued, the English sinking the Spanish flagship which lay in such shallow water that her upper works were still manned by arquebusiers even when she was resting on the bottom. There were other casualties on both sides, but when fire-ships were seen drifting down upon the *Jesus* Hawkins decided to abandon her in order to make a stand in the *Minion*. 'Our General with a loud and clear voice called unto us saying "God and St. George! Upon those traitorous villains and rescue the *Minion*!" ' Since Drake's *Judith* had the outer berth, he was in a better position to get clear. Hawkins shouted to him to make for the open sea, whither he would follow in the *Minion*, leaving the *Jesus* and four smaller ships to their fate. Apart from Grenville's *Revenge*, she was the only warship to fall into the hands of Spain during the whole course of the war.

Young Drake was only a spectator in this affair, his little ship being of small account. He anchored her out of range, awaiting Hawkins's escape, but the next morning he made sail for home on his own account. It is difficult to say why he did not heave to, in order to get in touch with those on board the *Minion*: we can only charitably suppose that the contrary winds which they encountered as soon as they reached the open sea made this difficult. One cannot say exactly what happened, but we know that after his return to England Hawkins complained that the younger man 'forsook us in our great misery'.

For the *Minion* was so overcrowded with those who escaped from the other ships that a hundred of them had to be put ashore on the uninhabited coast of Mexico. Of these, three managed to return to England in a French vessel having, as they averred, marched right across the unexplored American continent to Cape Breton. The rest fell into the hands of the Inquisition and it is worth examining their fate because it illustrates the dangers to which men like Drake were exposed, as well as the hate which Spain inspired in our seamen.

Records of their trials by the Inquisition have survived, so that the confessions extorted from them by thumb screws and 'brain washing' give a more detailed picture of this little group of men than of any other similar Elizabethans. Most of them recanted after floggings, abjured their heretical practices and wore the penitential yellow robe. Thus one mariner from Looe in Cornwall, aged twenty-six, was sentenced to two hundred lashes and six years in the galleys; another from Plymouth to two hundred lashes and eight years in the galleys. Only three were actually burned—two by the Mexican Inquisition, which ordered the more humane method of putting heretics to death by strangulation before burning. The third (Robert Barrett of Saltash, the master of the *Jesus*) was taken back to Seville, where he was burned in the market-place at a Spanish *auto da fé*. Hawkins did his best to obtain their release while the trials were going on, but it happened that Drake was off the coast on his raid of 1572, so that it was not a propitious time for clemency.

What happened at San Juan de Ulua left a deep impression on Drake's mind. He had been defeated and betrayed on his first command. Never again would he trust the word of a Spaniard. Revenge became his aim for the next ten years. When a Spaniard whom he took prisoner on his voyage round the world asked him what his intentions were, Drake replied, 'I am not going to stop until I have collected the two millions that my cousin John Hawkins lost at San Juan de Ulua'. It may well be doubted if ever Hawkins had two millions to lose, but the Spanish Viceroy's treachery had made an enemy of Drake for ever.

This disastrous voyage occurred when the international situation was deteriorating. Hawkins and Drake returned at the beginning of a year when the Protestant cause suffered many setbacks and the neutrality of England began to waver. The previous year Mary Queen of Scots had fled to England thereby creating a centre of disaffection. The Duke of Alva succeeded in supressing the rebellion in the Netherlands; Elizabeth thereupon arrested all the Spanish shipping she could. It was becoming obvious that an open breach with Spain could not long be delayed.

CHAPTER THREE

★

The Raid on the Mule Trains

John Hawkins made no more voyages to the Main for nearly twenty years. His career lay at home where, as Treasurer of the Navy, he became the chief architect of the fleet which defeated the Spanish Armada. But Drake had only just begun his career at sea. When he asked Burghley, the Lord Treasurer, for permission to sail on a voyage of reprisal his demand was refused, official policy still being set on maintaining friendly relations with Spain in spite of the darkening of the international scene: England was not yet strong enough to wage open war with a power which still dominated the world.

Drake was not the man to take 'no' for an answer. Though little is known about them, he sailed in 1570 and 1571 on secret voyages on his own account, chiefly with the aim of finding a hidden harbour from which he could attack the treasure of Peru and Panama as it was transported on the backs of mules across the isthmus. A suitable anchorage was found at Port Pheasant, perhaps the Golden Island from which a band of buccaneers set out, inspired by his example, a century later, and which is now called Caledonia Harbour after the Scottish Darien colony of 1697; at any rate it was somewhere to the south-east of Nombre de Dios, the chief port on the eastern coast, to which the mule trains delivered the silver in bars and quoits.

Vancouver

San Francisco
NEW
ALBION

VIRGINIA Roanoke

St. Augustine
FLORIDA

Vera Cruz
S. Juan de Ulua

MEXICO

HISPANIOLA
San Domingo

PUERTO RICO

Rio de la Hacha GUADALOUPE

Porto Bello
Nombre de Dios

Guatulco

Panama Cartagena
DARIEN

Cabo San
Francisco

PERU

Callao Lima

Arica

BRAZIL

Valparaiso

River Plate

San Julian

PATAGONIA

Straits of Magellan
Cape Horn

ELIZABETH
IS.

Drake's circumnavigation route ⟵   Drake Strait

Sketch Map of the New World and the Pacific

It was by his raid of 1572–3 that Drake made his name as the supremely successful corsair, a reputation which inspired generations of buccaneers in those seas. We are fortunate in having a detailed account of his proceedings published by his nephew in 1626. The title of the narrative (which is one of the most stirring ever written) runs as follows: *Sir Francis Drake Revived: calling upon this dull and effeminate age to follow his noble steps for gold and silver. By this memorable relation of the rare occurrences (never yet declared to the world) in a third voyage made by him into the West Indies, in the years 72 and 73 . . . by Philip Nichols, preacher. Reviewed by Sir Francis Drake himself before his death, and much holpen and enlarged by divers notes with his own hand here and there inserted.* Never a handy man with a pen, it is unlikely that Drake ever wrote a connected story of his own exploits, but the vividness of detail (the authenticity of which is confirmed from Spanish sources) can only have been provided by an eye-witness, and we know that he presented some sort of narrative of the raid to the Queen at a later date.

He sailed on 24th May, 1572, in the vessel *Pasco* (named after a Plymouth worthy and owned by the Hawkins family). She was of 70 tons, his brother John being in command of the still smaller *Swan* of 25 tons, in which Drake had crossed the ocean the previous year. Experience had taught him that rowing boats and 'dainty pinnaces' were required for river work, so these were shipped on board in parts ready for assembly at his destination.

The voyage out was uneventful, but when they landed at Port Pheasant they received a shock. Nailed to a tree was a leaden plate on which was written, '*Captain Drake, if you fortune to come to this port, make haste away, for the Spaniards which you had with you here last year have betrayed this place, and taken away all that you left here. I departed from hence this present 7 of July, 1572. Your very loving friend John Garret.*'

Garret was a Plymouth man who had been left on the coast the previous year. Notwithstanding his warning, Drake waited to assemble his pinnaces and then embarked for Nombre de Dios. Surprise being invariably his chief weapon, he wanted to attack the place before news of his arrival spread along the coast.

They landed at three o'clock in the morning. The seaward fortifications were surprised before the tolling of the town bell gave warning of an attack. Leaving a dozen men to guard the boats, and telling John Drake to take sixteen men to attack the treasure house in the rear, Drake himself marched the remainder up the main street, drums beating and trumpets echoing to make his puny force seem larger than it really was. The garrison were alerted and 'presented us with a jolly hot volley of shot' at the end of the street. A bullet hit Drake in the leg, but he concealed the wound from his men, urging them on to push of pike. The enemy were forced back into the market-place, where Drake compelled a prisoner to lead him to the doors of the King's treasure house, within which he could discern by candlelight 'a huge heap of silver of 70 foot in length, of 10 foot in breadth, and 12 foot height, piled up against the wall. Each bar was between 35 and 40 pounds weight. At sight hereof our Captain commanded straightly that none of us should touch a bar of silver, but stand upon our weapons, because the town was full of people.'

At that moment, when all the treasure of the Indies lay before him, a stroke of bad luck ruined everything. A thunderstorm broke, soaking their bowstrings and powder horns. There was a movement of fear among Drake's men, 'which our Captain perceiving told them that he had brought them to the mouth of the treasure house of the world, if they would want it. But as he stepped forward, his strength and sight failed him, and he began to faint for want of blood, which, as then we perceived, had in great quantity issued upon the sand out of a wound received in his leg.' Without him they could do nothing. In spite of his protests to carry away some of the gold, they hoisted him on to their shoulders and bore him away to the boats.

Another plan was now necessary. Drake knew that half-way across the isthmus there was a fort known as Venta Cruces, the Crosses Roadhouse, where the mule trains from Panama met those from the north before proceeding together down to the coast. To reach the place it was necessary to make contact with the Cimarrone Indians (Maroons for short), who were escaped slaves sworn to vengeance on their Spanish conquerors. Without native guides it would be impossible to traverse the swamps and forests of the lowlands. It is remarkable how, during the ensuing months, Drake won the confidence of these men by treating them honestly and generously, never failing to keep any promise he made to them.

Some time passed before this plan could be put into action. Parties occasionally cruised along the coast, preying upon any craft they encountered. In one such fight John Drake lost his life. Another brother, Joseph, died (as did many others), from yellow fever. Drake ordered his body to be cut up to see if any reason for his death could be found, but neither this nor the drug which the surgeon produced was of any avail: indeed, the surgeon died of his own cure.

Thirty men had died of fever before word came from the Maroons that the Plate fleet was expected at Nombre de Dios. The time was ripe for an attack on the mule trains as they made their way down to the coast to meet it. With eighteen Englishmen and thirty Maroons, Drake set out through the jungle to lay an ambush on the road half-way across the isthmus, leaving half a dozen men to guard the ships. Every day they marched from sunrise till four in the afternoon, when their guides made them huts of boughs thatched with leaves to sleep in. On the fourth day they climbed a high ridge on the crest of which was a tall tree in which the Indians had built a look-out post from which it was possible to see both the Atlantic and Pacific oceans. Drake climbed the tree to be the first Englishman to see the Pacific. Falling on his knees, he besought 'Almighty God of his goodness to give him life and leave to sail once in an English ship in that sea'. Eight years later his prayer was granted; but before that date his most trusted companion John Oxenham, had forestalled him in a crazy attempt to seize Panama with a handful of men. He was caught and hanged at Lima at the very time Drake was sailing up the coast on his voyage round the world.

Three days after this event Drake's party reached the spot where the ambush was to be laid. A scout informed him that the Treasurer of Lima was on his way down to the coast with a train of eight pack animals laden with golden quoits and one with jewels. Two other mule trains of a hundred animals followed him.

At the appointed time of night Drake and Oxenham lay in the long grass on either side of the road, the plan being for one party to seize the bridles of the leading mules while the other overcame any resistance. The night was so still that they could hear the deep bells of the mules sounding some way off. But as the animals approached 'one of our men called Robert Pike, having drunken too much *aqua vitae* without water, forgot himself . . . and when a cavalier, well mounted with his page running at his stirrup, passed by, unadvisably he rose up to see what he was; but the Cimarron (of better discretion) pulled him down, and lay upon him, that he might not discover them any more'. It was too late. In order to distinguish friend from foe in the darkness,

Drake had told his men to wear their shirts over their clothes. The outrider caught sight of a white figure rising from the long grass, put spurs to his horse and galloped off to warn the others.

Through the stupidity of a drunken man the whole plan miscarried. An attack was made later on Venta Cruces, which turned out to be a miserable hamlet yielding little loot. Drake's control over the Indians as well as over his own men is shown by the fact that not a woman had 'any wrong offered them, nor anything taken from them to the worth of a garter'.

He must have been in low spirits as he led his weary men back to the ships. The original attack on Nombre de Dios had failed; half the company were dead of fever; now the ambush had failed too. He had been on the coast over six months and there was little reward to show for all their toil in this steaming climate. Only his invincible powers of leadership had maintained the morale of the men, but without material gain that could not be kept up much longer. Fortunately the Plate fleet was still off the coast and at this juncture his force was strengthened by the arrival of the fine 80-ton ship of a Huguenot corsair, Captain La Testu, fresh from France and seething with anger over the massacre of St. Bartholomew's Eve at Paris.

Early in March it was decided that twenty Frenchmen under La Testu and fifteen English under Drake should make another attempt to intercept the mule trains, this time at a point nearer Nombre de Dios, using the pinnaces to get as far as possible up the river which ran five leagues from the city. Once more they hid themselves by the roadside. Once more they heard the bells of the approaching mule trains.

This time the plan succeeded. The leading animals were seized, the guards riding off to give the alarm in the town

which was only a mile away. As many bars of silver and
quoits of gold as Drake's men could carry were stripped off
the mules, the rest of the treasure (amounting to fifteen tons
of silver) being hastily buried for a later visit. Unfortunately
another drunken man, this time a Frenchman, led to its
discovery by the Spaniards: having strayed from the party
returning to the boats, the man was captured and confessed
under torture. Captain La Testu was also left behind by
reason of a severe wound; he too was found and killed by
the enemy.

When Drake reached the river he was appalled to see
Spanish craft there instead of his familiar pinnaces. He must
get back to the big ships before they were surprised, so a
raft was hastily made and using a sapling for an oar he and
three others drifted down stream for six hours, up to their
waists in water with the sun beating down upon their heads.
Rounding a bend in the river they caught sight of the pinnaces bearing up in their direction. As he was hauled on
board anxious inquiries were made about the rest of the
party. He never could resist a joke, so he replied coldly at
first and then 'to fill them with joy, took out of his bosom
a quoit of gold, thanking God that our voyage was made'.
It is true that when they returned to the place where they
had hidden the treasure they found that the Spaniards had
dug it up, but they were able to recover thirteen bars of
silver and several quoits of gold—150,000 *pesos* worth,
according to the Spanish inventory.

He left Port Pheasant as soon as he could, sailing past
Cartagena in full view of the ships at anchor there with the
flag of St. George at his maintop. He loved to put on a
brave show, but one of his two ships was in no condition to
cross the ocean. So a better ship, though only of 25 tons,
was seized, laden with hogs, hens and honey, the latter
being especially welcome to these weather-beaten adven-

turers. Having spent a week careening his ships, paying their bottoms with tallow, burning the pinnaces which had served them so well and rewarding the Indians for their help, Drake and his band of sunburned buccaneers sailed for home.

Twenty-three days later, on Sunday, 9th August, 1573, they anchored in Plymouth Sound. It was sermon time and all good people were in church. But when the news spread that Drake was back the congregations ran out of the churches to welcome him, 'so that very few or none remained with the preacher'.

CHAPTER FOUR

*

Voyage Round the World: Atlantic

For three years after Drake's return from the Spanish Main we have no certain knowledge of his movements. There is a hint that the success of his raid aroused so much 'envy' in England that he thought it wiser to betake himself to Ireland; in other words, he was anxious to avoid the legal proceedings taken against him by the Spanish Ambassador. At all events we know that in 1575 he was in the pay of the Earl of Essex engaged in military operations in Antrim.

It was here that he met the man who caused the most tragic quarrel in his life. Thomas Doughty was a soldier, a scholar and a man of somewhat higher social standing than Drake himself. He must have possessed considerable charm and no doubt flattered Drake by his attentions, though we know from other evidence that he was capable of underhand dealings. For three years the two men were close friends, and it may have been Doughty who introduced Drake to Sir Christopher Hatton, a rising courtier who knew the mysterious Dr. Dee, astrologer, mathematician and geographer, whose influence behind the scenes is discernible in almost every voyage of exploration from the time of Willoughby and Chancellor's attempt to find a North East Passage to Cathay in the last reign.

At the moment it was the north-western route which

engaged most attention, Frobisher sailing on his second voyage in that direction only a few months before Drake embarked on his circumnavigation. Another group, headed by Sir Richard Grenville, was interested in a southern route via the Straits of Magellan. A project along these lines, including the discovery of Terra Australis Incognita, generally supposed (on no evidence whatsoever) to stretch diagonally between Tierra del Fuego to somewhere south of New Guinea, was suggested at this time and Drake certainly knew of it, but it was shelved for political reasons.

In 1577, however, Mr. Secretary Walsingham got in touch with him because relations with Spain had deteriorated once more. Summoned to London to meet the Queen, Drake arrived too late at night to see her. Next morning (so he told some friends a few months later) 'coming to her presence, she said, "Drake, so it is that I would gladly be revenged on the King of Spain for divers injuries that I have received;" and said further that I was the only man that might do this exploit, and withal craved my advice therein; who told Her Majesty of the small good that was to be done in Spain (by a landing) but the only way was to annoy him by his Indies'.

Beyond that vague statement we shall never know precisely what his advice was. The reasons and the plans underlying his voyage are extremely perplexing, chiefly because so many people were implicated in them. Originally there must have been a revival of Grenville's plan to be carried out under Drake's leadership. A draft to this effect, signed by Burghley the Lord Treasurer, exists in which Drake is instructed to proceed by way of the Magellan Straits to the coast (presumably of Terra Australis) in latitude 30°. Having discovered if there was any prospect of trade in those parts, he was to return home by the same route. This project had the support of a syndicate including such important people as Leicester, Walsingham, Hatton, Sir William Winter (Surveyor of the Navy), John Hawkins (now Treasurer of the Navy), the Lord Admiral and Drake himself, who invested £1,000.

But at the private interview with the Queen all this was probably changed, with the connivance of Walsingham, into something far more aggressive. Whether Drake himself suggested a raid on the unprotected coasts of Peru, inspired by his vision of the Pacific six years previously, or whether it was the Queen who altered the original plan we do not know. Nor can we say for certain how much Burghley knew of the change of plan before Doughty betrayed it to him. As to the return route, this secret plan may have envisaged a search for the western exit of the North West Passage and a return through it—if it existed. But as there is evidence that when he was off South America Drake was still uncertain which way he was going to return, it seems likely that the first Englishman to circumnavigate the globe did not contemplate doing so when he embarked at Plymouth in the autumn of 1577.

Only once before in history had such a feat been achieved, and that was the voyage of Magellan's *Vittoria* in 1519–22. The grim record of their passage across the Pacific, when the crew was reduced to gnawing leather to save themselves from starvation, and the way their leader was murdered in the Philippines, can hardly have inspired Drake with confidence as he read the narrative, which is one of the few books which we know he had on board.

The last time he set sail he had been an adventurer bent on private revenge. Now he was a respectable privateer with the Queen's commission in his cabin (so he said). In view of the high political stakes involved, the voyage was ostensibly bound for Alexandria. If some of his companions knew better, they did not realize that Drake had been appointed sole commander and not, as was usually the case in such voyages, a leader who depended on their advice and consultation. This uncertainty about the extent of his powers may well have been at the root of the troubles which nearly wrecked the venture before they reached the Pacific.

As 'captain-general', Drake commanded the 'admiral' of a hundred tons, with fourteen guns mounted broadside and four more on the poop and fo'c'sle. When she sailed she was called the *Pelican*, but when he entered the Magellan Straits Drake changed her name to *Golden Hind* in honour of his patron, Sir Christopher Hatton, whose crest was a *hind trippant or*. No good picture of the ship exists, though there is a crude vignette of her at the bottom of a map drawn some years later to celebrate the voyage. Claims have been made that the contemporary ship model at Oxford is of the *Hind*, but this is doubtful. She was probably about seventy feet long, with a draught of nine or ten feet, so that she could easily be hauled up on some shelving beach for cleaning or repairs. But the great quantity of treasure which she took on board made her low in the water, with almost fatal consequences on the later stage of the voyage. John Winter, Sir William's nephew, commanded the *Elizabeth* of eighty tons, and John Thomas the *Marigold* of thirty. There was also a storeship of fifty tons with Drake's favourite name, *Swan*, and a pinnace of fifteen tons (under his old boatswain Tom Moone) which was exchanged for a Portuguese prize off the West Coast of Africa and named the *Christopher*; neither of these small vessels entered the Straits.

By modern standards they were tiny ships with only a hundred and sixty men on board, but they were well-found and well equipped 'for ornament and delight'. Determined to show that he was now no mere corsair, but a representative of the Queen, Drake carried with him 'expert musicians, rich furniture, all the vessels of his table, yea, many even belonging to the cook-room, being of pure silver, and divers shows of all sorts of curious workmanship'—possibly the 'dial' which we have described in a previous chapter. So we are told in *The World Encompassed*, which Drake's nephew (whose father sailed on this voyage) published in 1628, basing his narrative on the rough notes of Francis Fletcher, the 'preacher' or chaplain of the *Pelican*. His story is supplemented by the vivid, though hostile narrative of the mariners Cooke and Cliffe, who returned home before completing the voyage, and by the despatches of the Spanish prisoners whom Drake released. There is also an anonymous narrative printed in Hakluyt's great collection of *Principall Navigations*, which was the first to appear, but which omits many items of interest because it was heavily censored. By collating these accounts it is possible to fill in some of the gaps left by Drake's relative, who was understandably anxious to present the exploit in its most favourable light: there were many more debatable incidents in the course of this voyage than in the raid celebrated in his former book, *Sir Francis Drake Revived*. Even then it must be admitted that a great deal of what Drake intended, and in some cases what he actually did, is extremely problematical. The greatest loss is Drake's own journal.

The start was inauspicious. Having left Plymouth on 15th November, 1577, the worst gale in living memory blew up as soon as they were out of sight of land. The *Marigold* was blown on shore, and the *Pelican* dismasted. In order to repair the damage they had to put back to Plymouth, from which they finally departed on December 13th. Coasting down the west coast of Africa, they visited one of the Cape Verde Islands, where they made the acquaintance of the coconut tree, the milk of whose fruit 'being drunk, you shall not only find it very delicate and sweet, but most comfortable and cordial'.

Off these islands they took a few small prizes. In one of them Drake found the solution of his navigational difficulties in the person of Nuño da Silva, a Portuguese pilot of wide experience, though he had never been in the Pacific. He was perfectly willing to accompany Drake through the Straits and up the coast of South America, until he was allowed to join his compatriots on the coast of Guatemala. He later described the *Golden Hind* as 'well fitted out and furnished with very good masts, tackle and sails. She is a good sailor and the rudder governs her well.' To appreciate Drake's firmness of purpose and the risks he ran we have to remember not only the small size of his ships, but the fact that his only guides were the large-scale (and largely imaginary) map of the Pacific in Ortelius's new atlas, an unidentified Portugese chart, three books on the art of navigation, and a narrative of Magellan's voyage over fifty years ago. He may not have shared the terrors felt by many of his crew, who believed the traditional stories of the dangers of sailing south through the burning zone, but he could not fail to recollect that Magellan faced a mutiny among his crew before he reached the South Sea, or that he was killed by natives before the voyage was completed.

It is with obvious relief that Parson Fletcher reports that the stories of the burning zone were 'altogether false'; but he was apprehensive when, on 12th May, 1578, after crossing the Atlantic in fifty-four days, they sighted the coast of South America in latitude 33° S., somewhat north of the river Plate. The place was marked on the map as the Land of Demons, to the south of which lay Terra Gigantium. The natives did indeed look like devils, with their naked bodies daubed black and white, the feathers in their hair giving the appearance of horns. The Patagonians further south were certainly of huge stature and strength; if not exactly giants, they were just as unpleasant to encounter. A landing party was attacked with arrows and the master-gunner killed before Drake shot two of these 'old weather-beaten villains'.

After coasting down the shores of Patagonia they reached Port San Julian on June 20th. The first thing that Drake saw (for he was always in the first boat to go ashore) was the gibbet erected by Magellan and the mouldering skeletons of his mutineers. It was just the spot to be faced with the nearest to mutiny he ever came in his life.

The trouble had started in mid-Atlantic, when he lost his temper with Doughty, who had punished Thomas Drake (his younger brother) for rifling the booty taken off a prize. Unfortunately for Doughty, when his own baggage came to be searched other pilfered articles were found among his belongings. In vain he protested that they were presents. Drake swore by God's life that he should suffer for it. After that he seems to have developed an unreasoning suspicion of his former friend. Doughty and his brother were moved from ship to ship. As the weather grew worse Drake became convinced that they were responsible for it in some way. 'Thomas Doughty is a conjuror,' he affirmed, 'a seditious fellow, a very bad and lewd fellow, and his brother is a witch, a poisoner, and such a one as the world can judge of. I cannot tell you from whence he came, but from the devil I think.' By the time the ships reached San Julian both of them were held close prisoners in the hold, the rest of the crew being forbidden to speak to them.

Doughty does not seem to have realized how serious the situation had become, or what sort of a man Drake really was. He continued to talk flippantly about returning home, or at least of confining their activities to the Atlantic. All the ruthlessness which was in Drake's character determined him to stamp out any sign of opposition before it wrecked the voyage he was set on. He was a man of a formidable will when his mind was made up, and it was a dangerous moment to cross him.

As soon as they landed he put Doughty on trial for his life. Appointing himself both judge and prosecutor, he empanelled a jury of forty men and proceeded to arraign Doughty on a charge of treason. When the accused was brought before him he was charged in these words: 'You have here sought by divers means to discredit me to the great hindrance and overthrow of this voyage, besides other great matters where I have to charge you withal'. According to the formula of the law courts, he asked him how he would be tried.

'Why, good General', replied Doughty, 'let me live to come to my country. I will there be tried by Her Majesty's laws.'

'Nay, Thomas Doughty, I will here empanel a jury.'

'Why, General, I hope you will see your commission is good.'

'I warrant you,' answered Drake, his patience at an end, 'my commission is good enough. My masters, this fellow is full of prating. My masters, you that be my good friends, Thomas Hood, Gregory, you there, my masters, bind him.'

A witness confirmed that he had warned Drake of Doughty's treachery as they were walking in his garden at Plymouth. The accused admitted that Lord Burghley knew of the plan. 'How?' asked Drake.

'He had it from me.'

'Lo, my masters,' cried Drake, 'what this fellow hath done! God will have all his treacheries known, for Her Majesty gave me special commandment that of all men my Lord Treasurer should not know it, but see, his own breath hath betrayed him.'

Doughty was found guilty by the jury, though many doubted the legality of these proceedings. The verdict was enough for Drake: 'You shall not have to do with his life. Let me alone for that. . . . And now my masters,' he concluded, 'consider what a great voyage we are like to make, the like of which was never made out of England before, for by the same the worst in this fleet shall become a gentleman; and if this voyage go not forward, which I cannot see how possibly it should if this man live, what a reproach it will be, not only unto our country, but especially unto us, the very simplest here may consider of. Therefore, my masters, they that think this man worthy of death, let them with me hold up their hands, and they that think him not worthy to die hold down their hands.'

With such a direction to the jury the result was not in doubt. The strangest part about the proceedings is that until the execution forty-eight hours later the two men resumed their old terms of friendship. A few hours before the axe fell they took Communion together, dining afterwards 'at the same table as cheerfully in sobriety as ever in their lives they had done aforetime, each cheering up the other and taking their leaves by drinking to each other, as if some journey only had been in hand'. But when the axe fell it was Drake who lifted up the head with the cry, 'Lo! this is the end of traitors!'

Since he was determined to assert his authority, this was the moment to secure that unanimity among his men which the dangers ahead demanded. On the Sunday following he spoke to the assembled company in words which not only echo the accents of the living man, but which form the foundation of naval discipline on board ship from that day to this.

As the chaplain stepped forward to preach the sermon, Drake pushed him aside.

'Nay soft, Master Fletcher, I must preach this day myself, although I have small skill in preaching. Well, be all the company here, yea or not? Answer was made that they were all there. Then commanded he every ship's company severally to stand together, which was also done. Then said he, My masters, I am a very bad orator, for my bringing up hath not been in learning, but what so I shall here speak, let any man take good notice of, and let him write it down, for I will speak nothing but I will answer it in England, yea, and before Her Majesty.

'Thus it is, my masters, that we are far from our country and friends, we are compassed in on every side with our enemies, wherefore we are not to make small reckoning of a man, for we cannot have a man if we would give for him ten thousand pounds. Wherefore we must have these mutinies and discords that are grown up amongst us redressed, for by the life of God it doth even take my wits from me to think on it. Here is such a controversy between the gentlemen and the sailors, that it doth even make me mad to hear it. But, my masters, I must have it left, for I must have the gentlemen to haul and draw with the mariners, and the mariners with the gentlemen. What, let us show ourselves to be all of a company, and let us not give occasion to the enemy to rejoice at our decay and overthrow. I would know him that would refuse to set his hand to a rope, but I know that there is not any such here; and as gentlemen are very necessary for govern-ment's sake in the voyage, so I have shipped them for that, and to some further intent, and yet though I know sailors to be the most envious people of the world, and so unruly without government, yet may I not be without them.

'Also if there be any here willing to return home, let me understand of them, and here is the *Marigold*, a ship I can very well spare. I will furnish her to such as would return with the most credit I can give them, either to my letters or any way else; but let them take heed that they go homewards, for if I find them in my way I will surely sink them. Therefore you shall have time to consider hereof until to-morrow, for by my troth I must need be plain with you. I have taken that in hand that I know not in the world how to go through withal, it passeth my capacity, it hath even bereaved me of my wits to think on it.'

The nervous strain under which the man was suffering is plainly evident. Doughty had been his personal friend, and he had executed him. The voyage sailed at the Queen's behest, and he knew what happened to servants of Tudor monarchs if they failed. They were about to enter an unknown sea with a doubtful destination in a few small ships sparsely manned. To make his position perfectly clear, every officer was dismissed his ship. Not a word was heard from those wishing to return. After an interval Drake declared the incident closed: 'Many there are who deserve no other fate, but as I am a gentleman there shall no more die. And now my masters, let us consider what we have done. We have now set by the ears three mighty princes, as first Her Majesty, and then the Kings of Spain and Portugal; and if this voyage should not have good success, we should not only be a scorning or a reproachful scoffing stock unto our enemies, but also a great blot to our whole country for ever. And what triumph would it be to Spain and Portugal!'

After this appeal to their patriotism, every officer was reappointed to his post. A week later, having disposed of the smaller ships, he led the *Pelican* (now renamed *Golden Hind*), the *Elizabeth* and the *Marigold* into the Straits of Magellan.

CHAPTER FIVE

★

Voyage Round the World: Pacific

The passage of the dreaded straits must be accounted one of Drake's finest feats of navigation. Neither he nor his pilot had anything to guide them through that maze of islets and inlets except a large-scale map of the world. Yet they only took sixteen days to get through, whereas Magellan before them had taken thirty-seven days, and Cavendish, when he repeated Drake's exploit ten years later, took forty-nine; indeed, on Cavendish's second attempt he himself died of starvation in the straits and only the ship commanded by John Davis returned to tell the tale.

Furthermore, Drake's men knew so little about the climate of the southern hemisphere that since it was August they assumed it must be summer in those parts. In fact it was the very dead of the winter. Parson Fletcher was soon complaining of 'the nipping cold, the grisly sight of the cold and frozen mountains'. For sixteen days they sailed between mountains whose snowy tops reached into the clouds. Here and there they landed to kill and salt penguins (which they called geese) in order to supplement their provisions.

At last the ships emerged into the South Sea. Being as ignorant of the wind system as they were of the climate, they were surprised to encounter violent head winds which soon rose to gale force. They were in the latitudes of the Roaring Forties, which blow unchecked along the southern rim of the world. Was this, they complained, the *mare pacificum*? It was more like a *mare furiosum*. For over a month the gale continued to blow. Never can Drake's seamanship have been so severely tested. The *Marigold* went down with all hands, those on board the *Golden Hind* hearing the despairing cries of her crew as she was overwhelmed by mountainous seas. Winter in the *Elizabeth* parted company and after waiting three weeks at the mouth of the Straits for Drake (during which time he took possession of Tierra del Fuego in the Queen's name) he put before the wind in order, so he said, to sail for the Moluccas by an easterly route. Emerging from the Straits, his mutinous crew compelled him to turn north for home, where he arrived at Ilfracombe the following summer. Is this story, which has only recently come to light, an excuse for deserting Drake? If it is true, why did Drake evidently expect to find him further up the coast? Possibly Winter disapproved of the change of plan from one of exploration to one of piracy. All that can be said is that the reasons for his return form one of the insoluble problems of this voyage.

The *Golden Hind* was thus left alone in a tempestuous uncharted sea. How far south she was driven by the gale is another uncertainty, because for weeks on end it was impossible to take a sight of the sun. Probably it was to latitude 57°. The latitude of Cape Horn is 55° 58', but there is nothing to suggest that Drake was driven as far east as the Cape, which was not discovered until 1616. One important discovery he did make, and that was the existence of the strait between Tierra del Fuego and Antarctica which now bears his name. Hitherto geographers had supposed that the two were joined as part of the Great South Land, but now it was seen that 'the Atlantic Ocean and the South Sea meet in a large and free scope'.

Finding shelter from the gale under the lee of what he

supposed was the southernmost island (some say it was Henderson Island, others believe that it was a volcanic reef now submerged beneath the surface of the sea), Drake landed to claim it for his queen under the name of Elizabeth Island. Lying face downwards, he stretched his arms over the edge of the southernmost cliff in order to be able to say that he had been further south than any man. He always liked to brag, and his brags were usually justified.

On October 30th, the wind having abated, he was able to set course north. The climax of the voyage had now come. Ahead of him lay all the riches which formed the life-blood of the Spanish Empire, unprotected and awaiting the greatest corsair of all time, since no foreign ship had yet entered these waters. In spite of the battering which the *Hind* must have received in the recent gale, she was still well-found, well-armed and well-led. The hearts of her crew lifted as they entered warmer latitudes. Even when their hopes of rejoining the *Elizabeth* began to fade, the prospects of easy plunder reconciled them to their lonely situation.

Off Valparaiso they surprised their first vessel without a struggle. They silently came alongside a ship riding at anchor in the harbour. A boarding party led by Tom Moone climbed up the side, to be welcomed by the few Spaniards on board, who imagined they must be fellow countrymen. 'Down dog!' shouted Moone, as he laid about them with his cutlass to drive the crew below hatches. When all had been secured, the vessel was rifled. Twenty-five thousand *pesos* of fine gold were found on board, together with a great cross of emeralds, one of which, half a finger long, Drake determined to present to the Queen. The pilot, named John the Greek, was detained to guide them up the coast, but everyone else was set free.

There is no space here to describe in detail the astonishing voyage up the coast of Chile and Peru. Time and again towns and villages were raided without loss of life on either side. Though the behaviour of his men on shore was often barbarous, it was never cruel, nor did Drake himself fail to treat all his prisoners with punctilious courtesy. Slow-moving cargo vessels, as often as not carrying silver from the mines of Potosi or what was left of the treasure of the Incas, were overhauled, 'eased' of their burden, and sent on their way again. The thing became a joke. Thus one narrative tells how a landing party removed 4,000 ducats from a man who slept so soundly that they did not trouble to wake him. On another occasion, when a Spaniard was seen driving before him eight llamas each carrying 3,000 pieces of silver, 'we could not endure to see a gentleman Spaniard turned carrier, so we offered our services and became drovers, and almost as soon as he had parted from us we were come to our boats'.

At Arica silver bars the size of bricks, each weighing twenty pounds, were taken on board. At Callao, the port of Lima, thirteen vessels were seen in the harbour. Entering under cover of darkness, Drake anchored alongside one of them just as a ship came in from Panama. The customs boat which rowed out to make a routine visit mistook the *Hind* for the other ship. A voice called up to her out of the darkness to inquire her name. Drake told John the Greek to reply in Spanish that the ship belonged to one Michael Angelo of Chile. Thereupon one of the customs officers came up the side, but stumbling against one of the guns on deck he guessed she was a pirate ship and vanished over the side again. Those on board the Panama ship were alarmed and put to sea as quickly as possible, but Drake had already sent the pinnace in chase. She refused to strike her colours when hailed. Shots were fired until her crew thought better of their resistance, abandoned ship and rowed themselves ashore.

It was at Lima that Drake heard the news that the King of Portugal was dead and that the two empires were now united under the Spanish crown, thereby giving her the monopoly of the whole tropical world. What he did not learn was that his old companion in arms, John Oxenham, was on trial for his life in that very town. He knew that he had been taken prisoner, so he took every opportunity of sending messages to the Spanish authorities to spare his life, but it was of no avail. Some months later Oxenham and his companions were hanged. Evidence of what it meant to fall into the hands of the Inquisition was provided for the crew of the *Golden Hind* when they heard that an *auto da fé*, at which six men were burned at the stake, had been held a few days before their arrival.

The most important news was that a big vessel nicknamed the *Cacafuego*, or *Spitfire*, loaded with bullion, had left a fortnight before, bound for Panama. Without wasting time, Drake went in chase of a ship which the Spaniards themselves called 'the great glory of the South Sea'. As he piled on sail he offered a prize of a gold chain to the first look-out who should catch sight of her from the masthead. A week later, off Cape Francisco, a shrill voice claimed the reward. It was that of Drake's nephew, John, who sailed on this voyage as his page, but was captured on a later voyage which tried to repeat his uncle's success.

A vivid account of what happened next has survived from the pen of the master of the *Cacafuego*, San Juan de Anton; it is possible, indeed, that he was an Englishman whose real name was St. John of Hampton on account of many years' residence at Southampton.

When he first sighted the *Golden Hind* on the horizon at three o'clock in the afternoon he thought she was just another of the peaceful barks he passed on his way to Panama. She carried a lot of sail, but she did not seem to be gaining on him—the reason being that Drake resorted to an old pirate trick of hanging out wine pots astern as a drag. He was therefore surprised when she caught up with him just as darkness was beginning to fall. Leaning over the taffrail to have a look at her, he heard a shout—'Strike, Master Anton! If not, look out, for you will be sent to the bottom!'

'What old tub is that to order me to strike sail?' he replied. 'Come on board and do so yourself!'

A bos'n's whistle shrilled in the darkness. A trumpet sounded on the poop as the signal for a volley of arquebus shot. The big guns spoke and a chain-shot carried away the mizen mast of the *Cacafuego*. At the same moment the pinnace, which San Juan had not noticed stealing up on the port side, suddenly appeared, from which a boarding party of forty men scrambled up the side. So sudden was the attack that San Juan was the only man on deck when their leader appeared over the side to demand the surrender of the ship. He was seized and carried on board the *Hind*, where Drake met him with the words, 'Have patience, for such is the usage of war.'

He was treated with Drake's usual consideration during the next three days while his ship was searched in order 'to do him the kindness of freeing him of the care of those things with which his ship was laden . . . some fruit, conserves, sugar, meal and other victuals, and (that which was the especiallest cause of her heavy and low sailing) a certain quantity of jewels, thirteen chests of *reals* of plate, eighty pound weight in gold, twenty-six tons of uncoined silver, two very fair silver drinking bowls and the like trifles, valued in all at about 360,000 *pesos*'. Once he had rifled her holds, Drake could afford to be generous. Some of the cargo was restored; presents were made to San Juan and others; and both sides parted good friends as she was sent empty on her way.

Before he bid her farewell Drake gave San Juan a safe-conduct in the form of a letter to Winter, should he be so unlucky as to meet another Englishman in those seas.

'Master Winter, if it pleaseth God that you should chance to meet with this ship of Sant John de Anton, I pray you use him well, according to my word and promise given unto them, and if you want any thing that is in this ship of Sant John de Anton, I pray you pay them double the value for it, which I will satisfy again, and command your men not to do her any hurt; and what composition or agreement we have made, at my return to England I will by God's help perform, although I am in doubt that this letter will never come to your hands. Notwithstanding I am the man I have promised to be, beseeching God the Saviour of all the world to have us in his keeping, to whom only I give all honour, praise and glory. . . . Your sorrowful captain, whose heart is heavy for you, FRANCIS DRAKE.'

By this time it was clear that the news had spread that El Draque ('the dragon') was on the coast. Future captures might not be so easy. Nevertheless off Acapulco on the coast of Central America he was able to repeat with success the tactics employed against the *Cacafuego*. What took place is described in a letter from the captain of the ship, Don Francisco de Zarate, to the Viceroy of New Spain, the same Don Enriquez whom Drake had encountered at San Juan de Ulua. Just before dawn, he writes, 'I saw by moonlight a ship close alongside. Our steersman shouted that she should get out of the way. To this they made no answer, pretending to be asleep. The steersman then shouted louder, asking where the ship hailed from. They answered "From Peru". . . . Suddenly she crossed our poop, ordering us to strike sail and shooting with arquebuses at us. We thought this so much of a joke as it afterwards turned out to be serious.'

It seemed impossible in those peaceful waters to be attacked by such a small vessel. Drake had chosen his moment well. Only half a dozen men were awake on board the Spanish ship, and so, Don Francisco ruefully reports, 'they entered our ship with as little risk to themselves as though they were our friends'.

'I found Drake walking on the deck and, on approaching him, I kissed his hands. He received me with a show of kindness and took me to his cabin, where he bade me be seated and said, "I am a friend of those who tell me the truth, but with those who do not I get out of humour. Therefore you must tell me how much silver and gold does your ship carry?"

' "None, only some small plate I use and some cups."

'He kept silent for a while, then renewing the conversation asked if I knew your Excellency. I said, "Yes".

' "Well, it would give me greater joy to come across him than all the gold and silver of the Indies. You should see how the word of a gentleman should be kept." '

The memory of the treachery at San Juan de Ulua still rankled. But Drake soon got over his ill feeling and his disappointment that Zarate's ship had so little to offer. He was at pains to show that he knew how to behave as a gentleman. The next day was Sunday. Zarate was interested to see how the English celebrated the day by dressing ship over all (as we should say) with flags and banners, and assembling the ship's company for church parade, at which Drake led the singing of the psalms. Afterwards, when they had dined off silver plate to the sound of music, Zarate was able to take a closer look at the man: 'He is a man of about thirty-five years of age, low of stature, with a fair beard, and is one of the greatest mariners that sails the seas. His vessel is a galleon of nearly four hundred tons [an exaggeration] and is a perfect sailor. She is manned with a hundred men, all of an age for warfare. Each one takes particular pains to keep his arquebus clean. He treats them with affection, and they treat him with respect. . . . I managed to ascertain whether the General was well liked, and all said they adored him.' A few days later Zarate was sent peaceably upon his way.

Drake's last prize was a small galleon with a cargo of China goods—silk, porcelain, and a golden statuette of a falcon with an emerald in its breast. She was not the stately Manila galleon which his successors in the Pacific, from Cavendish in the sixteenth century to Anson in the eighteenth, took as their greatest prize, but she carried one treasure beyond price—a book of charts of the South Sea. It was this which enabled him to dispense with the services of Nuño da Silva, whom he put on shore at Guatulco with many assurances of friendship.

It was time to leave these civilized but hostile parts. The voyage was 'made' and Drake's thoughts turned for home; but by what route was he to get back? He could not return through the Straits of Magellan because he knew that a Spanish squadron had been sent to intercept him, nor did he relish the prospect of another encounter with Cape Horn weather. So he continued to sail north up the coast of Lower California beyond the confines of Spanish settlement. Much argument has been spent on what was in his mind at that time. Did he seriously expect to find a western exit of the North West Passage? Or, now that he had a chart of the Pacific in his hands, did he decide to pursue the chief end of the voyage in the minds of those who had put up the money—a visit to the Spice Islands?

As with the problem of his furthest point south, there is considerable discrepancy in the accounts of the most northerly latitude he reached. Like Captain Cook (who was the next Englishman to sight this coast on a similar quest two hundred years later), he was extraordinarily unlucky with the weather. Though it was midsummer, the account reads as if the ship was entering polar regions instead of the latitude of Vancouver. The further north they sailed the colder it got, and there was no sign of a passage home. In latitude 48° (42° according to another account) they turned back to look for a convenient harbour where they could refresh themselves and refit the ship before the long voyage across the Pacific. Where exactly they found this 'convenient and fit harborough' on June 17th is another debatable question. One account says it was in 38° 30', but as the thick weather continued we cannot rely too much on the accuracy of the observation. It was certainly somewhere near San Francisco, though the inhabitants of modern California would hardly recognize the unfriendly picture given of their state— 'the general squalidness and barrenness of the country, so that in the midst of their summer the snow hardly departeth even from their very doors, but is never taken away from their hills at all; hence come those thick mists and most stinking fogs'. Only the thick mists seem to be familiar in this account.

The traditional site of the landing is Drake's Bay, where the white cliffs suggested a name for the land which he took possession of in the Queen's name—New Albion. Others favour Bodega Bay further north. The Drake Navigators Guild, a band of San Francisco enthusiasts, has recently made further exhaustive research into the matter, their conclusion being that the creek beside which the *Golden Hind* was careened is Drake's Estero, an inlet of Drake's Bay, about twenty miles north of the Golden Gate.

Until recently all that was known of the ceremony (which was similar to that which took place on Elizabeth Island) was that Drake set up 'a plate of brass, fast nailed to a great and firm post . . . together with Her Highness' picture and arms in a piece of sixpence current English money, showing itself by a hole made of purpose through the plate'. In the year 1936 just such a plate, eight inches long by five wide, with a hole the size of a sixpence in the right-hand corner, was found near the San Quentin peninsula inside the Golden Gate which marks the entrance to San Francisco Bay. On the plate (the genuineness of which is still debated by some metallurgists) is engraved the following inscription:

BEE IT KNOWNE UNTO ALL MEN BY THESE PRESENTS
JUNE 17 1579
BY THE GRACE OF GOD AND IN THE NAME OF HERR
MAJESTY QUEEN ELIZABETH OF ENGLAND AND HERR
SUCCESSORS FOR EVER I TAKE POSSESSION OF THIS
KINGDOME WHOSE KING AND PEOPLE FREELY RESIGNE
THEIR RIGHT AND TITLE IN THE WHOLE LAND UNTO
HERR MAJESTIES KEEPING BY ME AN TO BEE
KNOWNE UNTO ALL MEN AS NOVA ALBION.
FRANCIS DRAKE.

Drake's reception by the Indians of those parts was extremely friendly, since they imagined these weather-beaten mariners were white gods from another world. There were the same long and tedious speeches in an unknown tongue which bored Cook on Vancouver Island, the same embarrassing submission of the tribal chiefs. Gifts were exchanged, those on the part of the Indians chiefly consisting of feathers and tobacco. Altogether, the country, in spite of its climate, was inviting enough, especially as 'there is no part of the earth here to be taken up wherein there is not some probable show of gold and silver'—a curious prophecy of the Californian gold rush of the nineteenth century.

But Drake's Protestant soul was shocked by the savage dances of the natives, the women tearing their faces with their nails until the blood ran down, while the men 'tried to worship us as gods'. When he had established a fortified camp near the shore, a counter-demonstration was staged to these 'bloody sacrifices' at which passages of the Bible were read aloud and psalms intoned; and the Indians, 'observing the end of every pause, with one voice cried "Oh!" greatly rejoicing in our exercises'.

Meanwhile the work of careening the ship was completed. On July 23rd the *Golden Hind* sailed for the Spice Islands, crossing the Pacific in sixty-eight days. A landfall was made at some islands which they called the Land of Thieves from the pilfering habits of the inhabitants. Magellan had done the same thing, though his Ladrones were Guam and Tinian, whereas Drake's were probably the Pelew group. Then coasting down the eastern side of the Philippines, they reached Ternate and Tidore in the Moluccas.

Since these were the fabled Spice Islands, Drake treated Sultan Babu with the utmost deference. On his part the Sultan gave the English ship a royal welcome, saluting them with an impressive parade of war canoes and inviting them to feasts on shore where they were presented with fruit and sago (another new tropical product, about which our narrator is less enthusiastic than he was about coconuts). The manner of the Sultan's entry made all that they heard about the riches of these parts seem true: 'The king at last came in guarded with twelve lances covered over with a rich canopy, with embossed gold. He was attired after the manner of the country, but more sumptuously than the rest. From his waist down to the ground was all cloth of gold, and the same very rich; his legs were bare, but on his feet were a pair of shoes made of Cordovan skin. In the attire of his head were finely wreathed hooped rings of gold, and about his neck he had a chain of perfect gold, the links whereof were great, and one fold double. On his fingers he had six very fair jewels, and sitting in his chair of state, at his right hand stood a page with a fan in his hand, breathing and gathering the air to the king. The fan was in length two feet and in breadth one foot, set with eight sapphires, richly embroidered and knit to a staff three feet in length, by the which the page did hold and move it.'

Negotiations for a trade treaty were made easier by the fact that the Sultan had recently quarrelled with the Portuguese and so had no objection to granting a monopoly of trade to England in return for Drake's gifts. Six tons of cloves were taken on board as a dividend on the first treaty ever signed by a British representative with an eastern potentate. A cup made out of a coconut mounted in silver, with a model of the ship on top, survives to this day as a memento of the occasion.

At an uninhabited island further south they stayed a month to clean the ship and refresh themselves, since a few of their number were suffering from what appears to have been scurvy. Compared with later Pacific voyagers—Anson in particular— Drake was as successful as Cook in keeping his men healthy, but old wounds and illnesses brought on by changes of climate or by deficiencies in their diet were bound to take their toll. It was a strange paradise in which the fifty-eight survivors found themselves. Succulent crayfish, coconuts and bananas formed their diet. At night fireflies ('fire-seeming worms flying in the air') made every twig look like a lighted candle. Bats as big as hens were more terrifying visitants.

On December 12th they departed, passing within sight of the Celebes. For three weeks they would make little headway on account of contrary winds, and they were in more dangerous waters than they knew. On 9th January, 1580, disaster very nearly overtook them. As the ship was passing through the straits between Peling and Sula, she struck a coral reef and remained fast even when the tide rose. The night was spent in terror, everyone commending himself to God 'to spill or save'. Next day, Communion having been celebrated, Drake took practical steps to lighten ship. It was a difficult decision to make because the ship lay low in the water, heavy with bullion in addition to her main armament. Something had to be thrown overboard, so it was decided to risk half the guns, half the water casks and three tons of cloves. At first this sacrifice made no difference, but at high water that afternoon the wind shifted and the ship heeled over, freeing the keel from the cleft which held her. As if by a miracle, she slid into deep water.

We know how Cook felt when a similar disaster occurred towards the end of his first voyage round the world: it was the only occasion when his habitually calm demeanour forsook him. Drake's more volatile temperament found vent in a violent quarrel with Parson Fletcher. The reason for the scene is obscure. Perhaps it was a remark in a sermon about their recent plight being a judgement on them for their sins, the ship lying unduly low in the water on account of the booty which they had taken. At any rate something which was said Drake regarded as tantamount to mutiny. Fletcher was dismissed the quarter-deck, chained by the leg to a hatch on the fo'c'sle and treated to an incredible sermon culminating in excommunication: Drake certainly had a high opinion of the authority of a captain on board his ship. Thereafter the parson was compelled to wear a band on his arm, on which were the words 'Francis Fletcher, the falsest knave that liveth'.

The remainder of the voyage was uneventful. They ran along the south coast of Java until a favourable monsoon carried them across the Indian Ocean to the Cape of Good Hope, 'a most stately thing, and the finest Cape we saw in the whole circumference of the earth'. Thence they made a fast passage home, calling only at Sierra Leone on their way north. They anchored in Plymouth Sound on 26th September, 1580, after a voyage lasting nearly three years.

The first question Drake is supposed to have asked the boat which rowed out to meet him was, 'Is the Queen alive?' With his hold packed with hundreds of thousands of pounds' worth of silver, gold and jewels, he was taking no chances. The *Golden Hind* anchored under the lee of what we call Drake's Island, her only contact with the shore being visits by the captain's wife, Mary, and the Mayor of Plymouth. After consulting the latter, a messenger—Brewer the trumpeter—was sent up to London to ask for orders. A week later the Queen's messenger arrived. Drake was to leave his ship where she lay and come to town at once. The local authorities were to see that the treasure was safely locked up in Saltash Castle.

To prove his case Drake took the precaution of bringing up to London several horseloads of gold and silver, not forgetting the fine emeralds which he wished to present to the Queen, well knowing her love of jewellery. Unfortunately no record exists of the journey of that extraordinary caravan across the wilds of Salisbury Plain, winding along the narrow Surrey lanes and crossing London Bridge surrounded by curious and enthusiastic crowds. Nor can we do more than guess at the pleasure with which the Queen saw the booty unloaded in the courtyard of Whitehall Palace. Here before her, and before the eyes of her Council, was the glittering evidence of the results of the voyage in which they had invested. No one knows the exact value of the treasure which Drake brought home. Probably it was a quarter of a million pounds sterling in Elizabethan currency, which may be multiplied by at least fifty to reach a modern equivalent. All we know is that it was enough to pay a dividend of £47 on every £1 invested.

The final scene in this unparalleled success story took

place when the *Hind* was brought round to Deptford near the royal palace at Greenwich to lodge the treasure in the Tower of London. All the rumours which had been flying about since Winter's return two summers ago with the story of Doughty's execution were stilled. A deaf ear was turned to the insistent protests of the Spanish Ambassador. Drake's 'name and fame', says a contemporary chronicler, 'became admirable in all places, the people swarming daily in the streets to behold him'.

To set the seal on the voyage the Queen herself visited the ship on 4th April, 1581. At the moment she was conducting one of her interminable courtships, this time with the Duke of Alençon, whose representative accompanied her on board. A banquet was served, after which she commanded Drake to kneel before her. Now, she said, she had a golden sword to strike off the head of the man whom the Spanish Ambassador called 'the master thief of the unknown world'. Then, turning to Alençon's representative, she handed him the sword, bidding him give the accolade to Sir Francis Drake, the first commander to circumnavigate the globe (since it was Del Cano, Magellan's lieutenant, who completed the first voyage round the world after his captain's death in the Philippines). This was the sword used by the Queen to knight Sir Francis Chichester after his solo voyage round the world in 1967.

For many years a visit to the *Golden Hind* was the favourite Sunday jaunt of Elizabethan Londoners. In time she fell to pieces, so that by the middle of the next century, when generations of tourists had helped themselves to mementoes of the most famous ship of a bygone age, nothing remained for posterity except two pieces of furniture made out of her timbers—a table in the hall of the Middle Temple, and a chair in the Bodleian Library at Oxford.

CHAPTER SIX

★

The Descent on the Indies

Drake's share of the profits from his voyage round the world was sufficient to enable him to establish himself (as did so many of his contemporaries) as a member of the landed gentry. His knighthood was the first step, the crest of his coat of arms being a ship surmounted on a globe; he seems to have added to the coat itself a wyvern, or water dragon, which was the crest of the Drakes of East Devon, a senior branch of the family, one of whose descendants became the mother of the Duke of Marlborough and hence the direct ancestor of Sir Winston Churchill.

The next step was to buy a house and land. In this transaction, as in those civil affairs in which he was involved for the next few years, he showed himself a keen business man. One of the oldest West-country families were the Grenvilles, who, at the time of the Dissolution of the Monasteries, bought from the Crown the Cistercian abbey of Buckland, a few miles north of Plymouth. The abbey was some two hundred and fifty years old and built, as was the habit of that order, in a remote spot. Sir Richard Grenville (grandfather of the captain of the *Revenge*) converted it into a comfortable country house and bought up bits of church property in the locality. Old Sir Richard was something of a poet at the court of Henry VIII, where he wrote some lines which express admirably the spirit of Drake's career:

Who seeks the way to win renown
Or flies with wings of high desire;
Who seeks to wear the laurel crown;
Or hath the mind that would aspire;
Let him his native soil eschew,
Let him go range and seek anew.

Drake was not on friendly terms with his grandson. The young Sir Richard must have been annoyed when his South Sea scheme was entrusted to Drake's leadership, and even more angry when, a few years later, Drake brought back the first colonists from his favourite project of Virginia. However, it was from Sir Richard that Drake bought Buckland Abbey in 1581. The deal was made through two other persons acting, it must be presumed, in Drake's name, and the price was £3,400, a lot of money in those days.

Here Drake's first wife Mary (whom he had married in 1569) died in 1583. His second wife, Elizabeth Sydenham, must have been an exceedingly pretty girl, if we may judge from her portrait, when he married her in 1585. She was also of a much higher social class than Mary Newman: she had been a maid of honour, and only Drake's rise in the social scale could have earned approval for the match. By neither wife did he have any children, so that his youngest brother inherited the place which has descended through generations of Drakes until in 1951 it became the property of the National Trust and was opened by Admiral Mountbatten as a Drake Museum. Here are preserved many personal relics of the admiral—his furniture and accounts, his seal and sword, even the flags of his ships and the bowl and drum traditionally connected with him. The drum is the most famous of these objects, the story being that the dying admiral told his men to hang it up in Plymouth church, whither he would return if it was beaten in time of danger; it has his coat of arms on it and at least it is the sort of drum which was used at that date.

As the most famous man in the country, Drake played a prominent part in local affairs during the few years when he was not on active service. In 1581 he became Mayor of Plymouth, in which capacity he earned the city's gratitude for improving the water supply. In 1583 he represented a Cornish borough in Parliament and was frequently in attendance at Court.

Towards the end of 1584 his services were required once more by the Crown. Elizabeth was still clinging to her policy of friendly relations with Spain, so that though Drake was actually commissioned in December 1584 to lead a combined military and naval expedition to the West Indies, it was not until Philip II seized all English shipping in Spanish ports the following summer that she finally agreed to launch an act of open war, though indeed war was never formally declared between England and Spain. What today we should call the 'cold war', which had been carried on by Drake and his followers ever since the disaster at San Juan de Ulua eighteen years before, now gave place to military operations sanctioned and promoted by the government. When Drake sailed in September 1585 the war with Spain, which continued until the end of the reign, had begun.

The expedition which he was chosen to lead was the biggest which left these shores for a hundred years. As soon as the news spread that he was fitting out at Plymouth men flocked 'with great jollity' to serve under such a famous commander. The Queen provided the two largest ships, in one of which—the *Elizabeth Bonaventure* of 600 tons—the admiral flew his flag. The remaining nineteen ships—apart from pinnaces—were provided by the city merchants of London and elsewhere. They were commanded by as choice a company as ever served: Christopher Carleill, Walsingham's son-in-law and a soldier of experience in Ireland and the Low Countries; Martin Frobisher, the bear-like seaman whose real interest lay in loot and fighting, though he had won fame by his three voyages in search of the North West Passage; Drake's brother Thomas, the inheritor of Buckland Abbey, his faithful old coxswain Tom Moone and his cousin Richard Hawkins, the son of Sir John, received their first commands. Even Sir Philip Sidney, the Queen's new favourite, tried to join at the last minute, but was hastily recalled to Court, only to lose his life on the field of Zutphen a year later. This force of 2,300 men was a very different matter from the small bands of adventurers which Drake had previously commanded. At last he was no longer a corsair but a commissioned commander-in-chief, and he was justifiably proud of the fact.

As was usual whenever he was in command, the some-what vague plan of operations was liberally interpreted as opportunity offered. Ostensibly he was told to free any ships remaining in Spanish ports, which provided him with an opportunity to sack the town of Vigo, the first home port in Spain to feel the lash of his wrath. After that he wasted little time on the coast because what he was really after was the treasure fleet returning laden with silver, pearls and emeralds, which was due home about this time of year. But as he made his way south into a lower latitude in order to intercept it he heard from a French corsair that he had missed it by twelve hours. So, having paid off an old score against the town of Santiago in the Cape Verde Islands, where one of the Hawkins family had been insulted, he stretched across the Atlantic to fall upon the West Indian colonies themselves. There was even talk of following this up by crossing the isthmus of Panama, but it now seems likely that his final destination was the new colony in Virginia promoted by Sir Richard Grenville and Sir Walter Raleigh.

The coast of what was to become after many vicissitudes the first British colony overseas had been explored the previous year by Captains Amadas and Barlow. After hearing their favourable report Raleigh and Grenville decided to develop their scheme of a settlement with the particular aim of providing a base for raiders operating in the Caribbean. The place was admirably suited to intercept the annual treasure fleet as it made its way homeward up the Gulf Stream, as Richard Hakluyt (their publicist) makes clear in his *Discourse on Western Planting*. The harbour at Roanoke was kept a close secret in case the Spaniards should attack it. The Queen approved the project, permitting Raleigh to name it 'Virginia' after her, and there can be little doubt that Drake knew what was afoot and what part he was to play in replenishing the colonists who sailed a few months before he did.

On reaching the West Indies Drake decided at a council of war to launch a surprise attack on Santo Domingo on the southern coast of Hispaniola (Haiti). Though this place had been the capital of the Spanish empire in the New World ever since Columbus had founded it, and was regarded as the chief jewel in Philip's colonial crown, it consisted of a mere five hundred houses inhabited by townsmen who lived in constant dread of a slave revolt or a raid by 'lutheran' corsairs. The fort guarding the harbour was one of the strongest in Christendom. Behind it rose the impressive buildings of the cathedral and several important monasteries. But as the inhabitants always visualized an attack from the sea, the walls of the city were not completed, part still being fenced with a cactus hedge. Beyond a few galleys in the harbour, there was at that date no Spanish naval force in the Caribbean, nor any regular army. The governor of Santo Domingo had at his disposal only five hundred arquebusiers and a hundred horse, apart from a militia provided by the townspeople. The sudden appearance of Drake's fleet in the road-stead took them by surprise. He had only to knock at the gates of the Spanish empire for them to fall in.

Only a commander of tactical genius could make it look as easy as that. On no other occasion in Drake's career does he appear to such advantage in his handling of the tactics of surprise and indirect approach. Wisely accepting the principle that a ship is no match for a fort, he landed Carleill with a thousand men at an unguarded spot some ten miles west of the city. Before dawn this force was on the march with band playing and standards flying, dividing into two bodies as they approached the sleeping city, one to take it in the rear and the other in the flank. Meanwhile Drake himself had returned off the harbour with his ships. The fort opened fire on them, but their shot fell short and by now the landing party was in action with the enemy on the open ground outside the walls. They pressed forward so resolutely that all opposition soon gave way before them. By five o'clock in the afternoon the standard of St. George was flying from the tower of the cathedral to notify Drake that the town was won. Whereupon all the ships 'shot off their ordnance for joy', the business being so easy, adds one of the logs, that it seemed as if 'the Spaniards gave us the town as a New Year's gift'.

For the next month Drake bargained with the governor over the ransom, while his men (assisted by galley slaves whom the Spaniards had unwisely released to fight what the authorities regarded as a common enemy) sacked the town more thoroughly than any Spanish town had ever been sacked before. Those of the inhabitants who had not fled were imprisoned in the cathedral crypt while negotiations continued between the humiliated *hidalgo* and the stocky self-confident seaman to the accompaniment of raging fires and crashing masonry. Drake began by demanding a million ducats. This was so obviously beyond the city's capacity to pay that he agreed to halve it, and then accepted a mere 25,000. To raise even that sum every inhabitant had to lay his personal treasure on the scales—plate, jewels, gold chains, ear-rings. In consideration of this sacrifice, the chief buildings were left standing, but their interiors were gutted. 'We burned all their images of wood,' writes a furious Protestant on board the *Primrose*, 'brake and destroyed all their fairest work within the churches, and we had in this town much plate, money and pearls hidden in wells and other places.' The only justification for such barbaric behaviour was that the town had not surrendered. It had been taken by assault, and on such occasions (as the Spanish were to afford terrible proofs in the Low Countries) any behaviour was permissible.

Considering the importance of the city, the booty was inconsiderable. Might not Cartagena on the mainland prove a richer prize? Drake knew it well, since he had often passed it by in his old raiding days. On 9th February 1586, he was off the town, sailing slowly past to examine the defences. The lie of the land seemed to favour the defenders. Cartagena is built on an island joined to the mainland by a bridge on one side, and by a narrow neck of land leading to a broad peninsula on the other. Lagoons lie behind it, the entrance to the inner anchorage (in which some galleys were moored) being protected by a chain and a blockhouse. The isthmus itself was fortified by trenches and a barrier of wine casks, but as Drake sailed along he noticed that the beach at the seaward end sloped sharply down to the surf, thereby affording dead ground from the fire of those in the trenches. Even more important was the fact that not so much as an earthwork defended the entrance to the outer lagoon. He would repeat his amphibious tactics at Santo Domingo: land Carleill and the troops on the tip of the peninsula, and send Frobisher with the smaller ships to make a diversion by bombarding the boom and its protective blockhouse.

Before it was light the soldiers had reached the trenches, wading through the surf to avoid the poisoned stakes which had been planted on the dead ground. 'Down went the butts of earth and pellmell came our swords and pikes together after our shot had first given a volley, even at the enemy's nose. Our pikes were somewhat longer than theirs and our bodies better armed, for very few of them wore armour.' Carleill himself struck down their standard bearer, and though Moone and a score of others were killed in the desperate struggle, the rest broke through and were soon racing the militia for the town gates. In vain a few officers tried to rally their men with cries of 'Close in, Spain! St. James and at them! They are heretics and few!' Someone was heard shouting 'Retire, gentlemen, for we are lost!'—possibly an Englishman speaking Spanish—and the defenders panicked. Only the governor remained at his post appealing in vain, 'Do not retreat, brothers, but fight!'

It was all over before noon, when Drake made his appearance in the market-place to take possession of the town. But once more he overestimated the wealth of the Indies. Many of the inhabitants had made off across the bridge with their valuables in their hands. The Admiral was in an angry mood, not only because his losses were greater than at Santo Domingo (and he felt Tom Moone's death keenly), but also because he found lying open on the governor's desk a despatch from the King of Spain which referred to him as a *corsario*. Now he was a commissioned high-ranking officer and he intended that all should know it. 'Because of this,' wrote a Spaniard who was present, 'he said many shameless things,' among others a demand for twice the ransom price. In his turn the bishop lost his temper and left the room declaring that no money should be paid at all. The governor, anxious for the city's safety, tried to beat down Drake's extortionate demands until, after a week's wrangling, he too withdrew from the negotiations. In the end, after Drake had threatened to blow the whole place up and had actually produced bombs to do so, the people prevailed on the governor to compound for 107,000 ducats (about £100,000 today) in bullion.

Far more serious than this comparatively small reward for so successful an exploit was the fact that disease—possibly yellow fever or cholera (since a prisoner admitted that he had been told to poison the water supply)—was beginning to take its toll. For two hundred years to come every expedition to the West Indies lost more men by disease than by enemy action. Unlike commanders such as Vernon and Wentworth in their attack in 1740 (at which date the memory of Drake's raid was still bright), Drake knew the importance of speed. He decided to get to sea again within a week. For this he has been criticised on the grounds that Cartagena would have afforded a base in the very heart of Spanish America. But there can be no doubt that he was right. He would have lost all his men if he stayed much longer, such was the ignorance of tropical medicine at that date. Nor did the Navy have enough ships to defend or supply such a distant place. Invasion was brewing at home, and was not the Roanoke colony designed by its promoters to afford just such a base in a more temperate latitude?

Since recently published documents make it pretty clear that Drake's ultimate object was the replenishment of this colony, he had every reason to make haste to the northward without pausing to attack the third big city in these parts, Havana. As they made their way round the west end of Cuba through the Florida channel they called in at various uninhabited islands in order to refresh themselves, for disease was now rife. The Admiral himself heartened his men by taking a hand in rolling the water butts up to the springs. 'I do wrong', says one of his companions, 'if I should forget the good example of the general at this place, who to encourage others took no less pains than the meanest.' The Spanish town of St. Augustine lay directly on their route, a base established to water the treasure fleet on its way home. Since, as Drake realized, it would be from this place that any attack on Virginia would be launched, it merited his attention. Once more Carleill landed with red flags flying to signify that no quarter would be given if he met with any resistance. It was 'a little town without walls, built of wooden houses' when they arrived. When they left it was a heap of ashes, though Drake took good care not to damage the Indian village lying close by.

On June 9th they reached the secret anchorage of Roanoke, no mean feat of navigation since he had no charts of that unknown part of the world. At first sight Ralph Lane the governor thought it was the promised relief ship from England, but as more and more ships came into view it was clearly Drake and all his company. As the latter knew that a permanent settlement was intended, he offered Lane the choice of a ship well loaded with supplies or a passage home. Lane chose the former, but that night a storm blew up, driving several vessels ashore. Others cut their cables, made for the open sea and never saw their consorts again until they reached England. The event so disheartened the colonists that one and all demanded passage home. It used to be said that these were the men who introduced tobacco into England, but it seems more likely that the plant was already known and all that these did was to introduce the Indian habit of smoking it in a pipe. Raleigh and his friends soon became heavy smokers, but whether Drake approved of 'the weed which purgeth superfluous phlegm and other gross humours' we cannot tell. One would like to think of him as the first naval officer to smoke a pipe on the bridge.

He was hardly out of sight of land when the vessel sent out by Raleigh arrived to find the place deserted. Grenville himself arrived a few weeks later to find an empty fort, two corpses hanging from a tree and an Indian princess, who told him how the colonists had been taken off by Drake. Thus it was that the man who above all others needed a base on which to build the structure of sea power in those seas was the unwitting instrument of the destruction of England's first colonial venture. It was not for another twenty years that a permanent settlement was made in Virginia.

Drake's descent on the Indies stands pre-eminent in the annals of war as an illustration of the tactics of an amphibious expedition, notably in the use of surprise and sudden attack. If it was not as financially rewarding as he had hoped (he seems to have been actually out of pocket himself when all claims had been met) that was partly because he missed the treasure fleet by sheer bad luck, and partly because he overestimated the wealth of the Spanish colonies. But he had shown how vulnerable the Spanish empire really was, so that he forced Philip to strengthen its defences at enormous expense, thereby ruining his credit in Europe. It was only when Drake revisited these parts ten years later on his last tragic voyage that he realized what he had done. By that date the Indies were well defended, as he found to his cost. One attack after another was beaten off where ten years earlier all would have been overthrown, and he died a disappointed man on the scene of his earlier triumphs.

At the moment, however, it looked as if the war had begun with a resounding success. As he wrote to Burghley shortly after his return, 'My very good Lord, there is now a very great gap opened, very little to the liking of the King of Spain. God work it all to His glory.'

★

Singeing the King of Spain's Beard

The most important news at the time of his return was that of the Babington Plot to assassinate the Queen and place Mary, Queen of Scots, on the throne. It was proved that Mary had full knowledge of the plot, with the consequence that she was executed the following year. With that event, taken in conjunction with Drake's open act of war and Elizabeth's assistance to the Dutch rebels, the invasion of England became imminent. News out of Spain spoke of intensive preparations for the 'Enterprise of England' in all the chief ports. For the first time Elizabeth was called on to make a firm strategic decision, and this she was incapable of doing. Naval power was such a new thing in these islands that no one except Drake realized its potentialities, or the way in which it should be exercised. Elizabeth continued to play for time by disowning Drake, but by this date no one believed her and wiser counsels prevailed on her to take the first steps in mobilizing her forces.

Drake was put in command of a fleet, but its character was of the usual joint-stock kind partly because the Queen never spent a penny more than was absolutely necessary, relying on her subjects to do the work of the Crown, and partly because this method seemed to provide a loophole should she have to disavow him once more. However, there could be no question that Drake was her admiral, that his flagship was once more the Royal ship *Elizabeth Bonaventure*, that his vice-admiral was an old officer of the Crown, William Borough, the Clerk of the Ships, and that the latter's ship, the *Golden Lion* was, together with the *Dreadnought* and the *Rainbow*, a Royal ship. But Drake himself fitted out four others at his own expense, the Lord Admiral provided one more, and the Levant merchants equipped the London squadron of seven ships which contracted to serve under Drake's leadership. As on previous expeditions, the undertaking was half official and half a business proposition.

Drake's instructions were equally ambiguous. In view of the menacing attitude of Spain he was told 'to prevent or withstand any enterprise as might be attempted against her Highness' dominions'. How he was to do it was left to him to decide, though he was given permission 'to distress the (enemy) ships within the harbours themselves'. At the last moment, however, the Queen drew back. A special messenger was sent down to Plymouth to inform Drake that he must 'forbear to enter forcibly into any of the King's ports or havens, or to offer any violence to any of his towns or shipping within harbours, or to do any act of hostility upon the land'.

But Drake had already sailed when the messenger reached Plymouth, nor could the pinnace which took the message to sea make contact with him—a somewhat suspicious circumstance. Perhaps he knew enough about the Queen by now to realize that she would have second thoughts which would ruin his plans. At any rate, subsequent events during that cruise in the summer of 1587 contravened every detail of her unhappy afterthought.

He sailed in the highest spirits, to judge from the first of his vivid despatches to Walsingham, his particular friend at Court. He professed himself well pleased with his officers and men, the former (Fenner, Borough and Bellingham) 'very discreet, honest and most sufficient', the latter 'all members of one body to stand for our gracious Queen and country against Antichrist and his members. . . . The wind commands me away. Our ship is under sail. . . . Haste! From abroad her Majesty's good ship, the *Elizabeth Bonaventure* this 2nd April, 1587.'

In a few days the fleet was off Cadiz, the white buildings of the town on the peninsula standing up clear against the roadstead beyond. From this outer harbour a narrow passage called the Puntal passage led into the inner harbour and the dockyard of Port Royal. Drake could see how the place was packed with shipping—galleons, caravels, barks, transports—all protected by a dozen galleys of the royal fleet. The wind served, so without hesitation, and in spite of the protests of his vice-admiral who was brought up to have an exaggerated idea of the importance of galleys, he led straight in to the attack on April 16th.

It was as if a pack of wolves had leapt into a sheepfold. Everything was in confusion as the English ships fired and boarded as they pleased. Some vessels cut their cables to run for refuge into the inner harbour. The galleys with their shallow draught thought it best to withdraw under the guns of the forts. Lying far up the inner harbour, Drake could see the great galleon which was to be the flagship of the Marquis of Santa Cruz, the admiral-designate for the Enterprise of England on account of his victory in the Azores over a French fleet a few years earlier. The temptation to destroy her was too much for Drake. Borough, on the other hand, having already protested against the attack on the outer harbour, now refused to follow him through the Puntal passage into confined waters where, if the wind dropped, they would be at the mercy of the galleys. But once more the latter failed to play their part because Drake's broadsides proved the superiority of the fire power of the galleon over the galley with her puny bow chasers. Santa Cruz's flagship was sent up in flames, the cargoes of the huddled merchant vessels rifled for fruit, wine and oil, twenty-four ships (Drake says thirty-seven) were burnt and six prizes taken in tow.

And then the wind dropped. The galleys made another half-hearted attack, but they were kept out of range, as were the fireships which were launched against the English, until, at two o'clock in the morning, a land breeze sprang up with the dawn to carry them out to the safety of the open sea. 'Having performed this notable service, we came out of the Road of Cadiz on the Friday morning with very little loss not worth the mentioning.'

Drake, as he put it, had only 'singed the King of Spain's beard'. He had not destroyed the Armada which was, he was told, gathering in all the ports of Spain, on the Biscayan coast, at Corunna and at Lisbon. From Cartagena and the Mediterranean ports a strong squadron was expected in the Gut of Gibraltar any day now. Drake at once proceeded south off Cape St. Vincent to intercept it, but it was not long before he realized that he was too late. With his strategic insight he knew the value of a base covering the straits of Gibraltar, and the towns of Lagos and Sagres (where Henry the Navigator had established the first navigational school in Europe) on the St. Vincent peninsula were the obvious choice. Though a force of a thousand men was landed on the beach at Lagos, the town was too strongly protected to be taken by assault. Another landing was made at Sagres, where Drake himself led the attack on the battlemented castle, although he was without the heavy artillery necessary for a siege. Faggots were piled before the main gate and pitch poured on to them. Under a hail of musketry the 'forlorn' or storming party forced a breach and within two hours a flag of surrender was hung out on the walls.

These rapid events were altogether too much for William Borough, the vice-admiral. We have seen how he refused to follow Drake's lead at Cadiz. Ever since they sailed from home he had disapproved of the admiral's methods. With a long and honourable record of service behind him in the Queen's navy, he was doubtless piqued at having to serve under an ex-pirate. As Clerk of the Ships he was unwilling to run the risks which Drake so serenely took. Furthermore it was the custom of the service that senior officers were consulted before any line of action was adopted. Drake's first council of war showed that he had made up his mind already, so that the proceedings were farcical. It was no good pointing out to him that, according to current theories on the art of war, galleys in confined waters were supposedly supreme. It was useless protesting that landings were prohibited, because Drake sailed before he was officially informed of this restriction. Borough seems to have known of it, so he felt that it was his duty to put his protests in writing. Referring to Drake's manner of holding councils of war, he writes: 'This manner of assemblies are far from the purpose, and not such as in reason they ought to be. You also neglected giving instructions to the fleet in time and sort as they ought to have had, for which I have been sorry; but I have found you always so wedded to your own opinions and will that you rather disliked, and showed that it were offensive to you, that any should give you advice on anything.' He continues for ten pages to recite his own record of service to impress on Drake his importance and to protest against the attack on Sagres. 'I pray you,' he concludes, 'take this in good part, as I mean it; for I protest before God I do it to no other end, but in discharge of my duty towards her Majesty and the service, and of good will and well-meaning towards you.'

Drake was in no mood for this sort of thing. Borough's

obstructionism, however much he protested that he did it for the highest reasons, reminded him of Doughty. As before, he was far too quick to smell mutiny where an honest difference of opinion was intended. If a subordinate disobeyed orders, he must suffer for it, no matter how important a person he was. Borough hastened to apologize in a short note which opens with the words, 'I am sorry that you make such construction of my letter. I protest I did it only in discharge of my duty for the better performance of her Majesty's service'. Drake was a violent person when thwarted, as we have seen. Convinced that he knew better than William Borough how to perform such a service, he decided to have done with his vice-admiral. Borough was told to confine himself to his cabin and consider himself under arrest. There, remembering what happened at Port San Julian, the poor man wrote a lengthy complaint to Walsingham which he concludes by saying that he considered himself (like Malvolio) 'greatly abused . . . expecting daily when the Admiral would have executed upon me his bloodthirsty desire as he did upon Doughty'. At a court martial held a few days later he was, indeed, sentenced to death, the execution of his sentence being delayed until they reached England.

To return to matters of greater moment. Lisbon, it was obvious, was the centre of warlike preparations, so it was north to Lisbon that Drake now took his fleet. At that date it was the most heavily fortified port in the world. Since the crown of Portugal had been united with that of Spain, the place had been transformed into the chief western base of the Spanish navy. One glimpse of the fortifications at the mouth of the Tagus showed Drake that another attack such as that on Cadiz was out of the question. The risks he took were always calculated risks: this was sheer impossibility. The wind having dropped, he lay off the mouth of the river hoping that the galleys within would come out to attack him. But they were taking no chances to repeat the fiasco of the galley attack at Cadiz. 'The Marquis of Santa Cruz,' complained Drake, 'seeing us chase his ships ashore was content to suffer us there quietly to tarry and never charged us with one cannon shot.' He tried baiting the Spanish admiral with challenges to come out and fight, but Santa Cruz either could not or would not reply.

So, when a northerly gale sprang up, Drake put before it in order to cruise between Cape St. Vincent and Cape Trafalgar once more. A great deal of small coastal craft was destroyed, which had an unlooked-for effect when the Armada sailed the next year. Many of the vessels were carrying staves which the coopers at Lisbon were to make into water casks. By destroying their cargoes Drake ensured that the Armada sailed short of water, a shortage which was partly responsible for the disaster which finally overtook it.

One of his last despatches to Walsingham, dated 'from her Majesty's good ship the *Elizabeth Bonaventure* now riding at Cape Sagres this 17th May, 1587', concludes with a sentence which has become famous. Having told him the Lisbon news, Drake adds the following reflection: 'There must be a beginning of any great matter, but the continuing unto the end until it be thoroughly finished yields the true glory. If Hannibal had followed his victories, it is thought by many he had never been taken by Scipio.' In 1941, during the darkest hours of the late war, an army chaplain transformed the first sentence into the noble prayer which is now generally known throughout the Navy as Drake's Prayer: 'O Lord God, when thou givest to thy servants to endeavour any great matter, grant us also to know that it is not the beginning, but the continuing of the same unto the end, until it be thoroughly finished, which yieldeth the true glory.'

A few days after sending that despatch Drake moved suddenly west to the Azores. It was rumoured that a great carrack, the largest type of merchant ship afloat, was due there, fully laden on her way back from the East Indies. The prospect of what Drake liked to call 'some little comfortable dew from Heaven' was alluring, now that offensive operations off the Spanish coast were at an end. His men wanted to go home now that their service was no longer required, but when he told them of the quarry he had in mind there were no more complaints.

Sixteen days later they saw her, coming straight towards them, dipping her flags as a signal to their ships to show their colours. 'But we,' writes an eye-witness, 'knowing what she was, would put out no flag until we were within shot of her, when we hanged out flags, streamers and pendants, that she might be out of doubt what we were. Which done, we hailed her with cannon shot; and having shot her through divers times, she shot at us. Then we began to ply her hotly, our fly boat and one of our pinnaces lying athwart her hause, at whom she shot and threw fireworks, but did them no harm.' Seeing that she was about to be boarded and that she was trapped by a much superior force, she surrendered without further resistance.

The *San Felipe*, as she was called, was the biggest ship Drake ever captured. Only three such carracks were taken in the course of the war. So valuable was she that it is said that the project of an English East India Company was first mooted when her cargo revealed the wealth which was to be found in the East. To give a few examples from her inventory: 6,573 pieces of calico, 780 bundles of Chinese silk, carpets, taffetas, sarsenets, lawns in great quantity, 420 bales of indigo, 330 tons of pepper and more of cinnamon, maize, ebony and saltpetre, in all worth £108,049, apart from the value of the vessel and a casket of jewels which was found on board. The richest cargo ever taken was the *Madre de Dios* in 1592, valued at £140,000. The *San Felipe's* total value was £1849 13s. 11d., which was originally divided between the Queen, the Lord Admiral, the merchants who financed the London ships and Drake himself, whose share was £18,275. In the end the Queen sold her share to the merchants aud Drake for £50,000.

The carrack must have dwarfed the other ships of his squadron as she was convoyed home in triumph. His three months' cruise off the Spanish coast was the most brilliant of all his expeditions and the capture of the carrack a fitting reward to the climax of his career as an independent commander. The conduct of his operations revealed his consummate tactical skill, the finest example, Sir Julian Corbett calls it, 'of how a small well-handled fleet, acting on a nicely timed offensive, may paralyse the mobilization of an overwhelming force'.

But the immediate sequel proved that, however much he might swell with justifiable pride at the success of his exploits, and flourish caskets of jewels from the *San Felipe* to assuage those in high office who disapproved of the highhanded way in which he interpreted his instructions as a servant of the Crown, there were some whose integrity was unassailable. For justice, in his view, was not done upon Borough.

The vice-admiral, it will be recalled, returned home under sentence of death passed at a court martial held on board the *Elizabeth Bonaventure*. We have seen how, in the case of Doughty, Drake's conception of leadership was far different from that of his contemporaries. He had made his own way in the world by his sturdy independence, or, to put the matter another way, by his consistant refusal to allow any obstacle, whether fort or man, to stand in his way. He was impatient of any form of timidity or conservatism. In his view we were, and had been for some time, at war with Spain, which he regarded as the cause of Antichrist. The success of his tactics depended on speed and surprise, which would be wrecked by hesitation in any form. He was, moreover, a man of a strong and arbitrary will, whom it was dangerous to cross. What both Doughty and Borough failed to realize was that argument with such a man was tantamount to mutiny.

The legality of courts martial was extremely doubtful at that date. What happened at Port San Julian was glossed over and forgotten. What happened off Cape St. Vincent was a more serious matter. Borough had an honourable record as a naval administrator and as a naval commander: he represented the professional navy, as compared with the freebooters like Drake and Frobisher. Compared with Walsingham, Lord Burghley had never been a personal admirer of Drake, however much he may have valued his services. He was determined to have the affair re-tried on the return of the fleet, nor did the Queen intervene. Drake seems to have been genuinely surprised that the case was thus reopened, because he had always been of the opinion that a commander on active service, be he captain of a ship or admiral of a fleet, must have supreme power. He might have exceeded his instructions in landing on Cape St. Vincent, but the success of the raid had been so great that he thought that would be overlooked.

So he drew up a long list of articles indicting Borough on various counts. The vice-admiral contested the charges and even accused him of suborning the witnesses. Thus to the third count—'that Mr. Borough was so afraid that he could not tell where to ride with the ship'—he replied by showing that he had been under fire as long as any other commander in the fleet. It was equally untrue, he said, that he had ever promoted a mutiny on board the *Lion* to further his own ends and compel the fleet to return: 'As I hope to be saved by the blood of Christ, I did neither know, think or imagine of any such matter of this mutiny until it brake out.' At Cadiz, affirmed Drake, 'Mr. Borough came to the General in trembling sort, uttering most fearfully these words, How the ship whereof he was captain was hit, and also said what if one of the Queen's ships' masts should be hit, what danger were we in' (three witnesses). Borough brought twenty witnesses to testify that nothing of the sort occurred, but that he had merely visited the flagship to obtain some victuals. A further batch of witnesses declared that there had been no quarrel between the two men until Borough's protest was written. In sum, Drake's charges of cowardice and mutiny were found not proven, his complaints of desertion in face of the enemy were reduced to a mere excess of caution.

Throughout this unhappy affair he appears at his worst—implacable, vindictive, even dishonest. To Drake's chagrin, Borough was not merely acquitted but confirmed in his office and later promoted Comptroller of the Navy, though it is true that during the Armada campaign he was merely appointed to the command of a galley (the only one in the service) in order to make a survey of the Thames. Drake himself was reprimanded by the Lord Treasurer for the 'indiscreet brags and opprobrious words' which he had used to challenge the Marquis of Santa Cruz. Official policy being to avert rather than precipitate war, Drake's landings on Spanish soil and these personal insults to the Spanish navy were, in Burghley's opinion, unforgivable.

But this personal vendetta was a matter of minor importance compared with the danger under the shadow of which England now lay. Spain was arming. Drake might have postponed the sailing of the Invincible Armada by a few months, but no one doubted that the Enterprise of England would go forward. In spite of these troubles at Court, it was to Sir Francis Drake that all men looked for their defence. The finest hour was at hand.

CHAPTER EIGHT

★

The Defeat of the Spanish Armada

It was the general opinion in England that the Spanish Armada would sail in the autumn of 1587. For that reason Drake's armament was kept in being and steps were taken to mobilize some sort of an army to oppose any landings that might be attempted, Leicester, Raleigh and Grenville taking the lead in these preparations. But as the months wore on the threat of invasion receded. Full credit had not been given to Drake's raid on the Spanish coast. The extent to which he had dislocated preparations, even if he had not destroyed the main body of the Spanish fleet, was not realized at the time.

The death of the Marquis of Santa Cruz early in the new year further delayed the expedition. The command was given to the King's cousin, Don Alfonso Perez de Guzman el Bueno, the Duke of Medina Sidonia. He did his best to excuse himself from this unwelcome honour, on the grounds that, unlike Santa Cruz, he was little experienced in maritime affairs, but the hierarchical structure of Spanish society demanded that some great nobleman should be placed at the head of the biggest fleet Spain ever sent to sea, it being understood that he would rely on the advice of the professional sailors who accompanied him—Recalde, Oquendo, and Don Diego Flores de Valdes, the last of whom sailed as captain of the fleet until he became Drake's prisoner.

The admirals had been collecting their shipping in the various ports of Spain, so that when the fleet sailed it was organized into provincial squadrons, those of Portugal, Biscay, Guipuzcoa, Andalusia and the Levant. It was primarily a fleet of warships convoying a large number of transports loaded with cavalry, soldiers, guns and horses, in order to make contact with the Duke of Parma in the Low Countries, who commanded the finest army in Europe consisting of some 19,000 men. Sidonia's objective was to anchor off what Philip called the Cape of Margate (which Englishmen called the Downs), whence he was to consult with Parma how best to launch an invasion up the Thames with London as their final aim. In case of bad weather he might take possession of the Isle of Wight, but Margate, not Calais (as it turned out) was his goal. As in the case of Napoleon's proposed invasion of these islands, English seamen were much less alarmed than those on shore at the prospect. A wave of panic and hatred of foreigners, inflamed by Protestant preachers from their pulpits, swept the country that summer. But Drake would have approved St. Vincent's remark that he could not guarantee Napoleon would not land, all that he was sure of was that he could not come by sea. Drake never had a high opinion of Spanish seamanship. It was Parma's troops and the chance of a surprise landing on their part which alarmed him, though he well appreciated the difficulties of embarking large numbers of men, under circumstances which neither Philip nor Napoleon nor Hitler ever seriously considered, in the face of an undefeated hostile fleet.

This is not the place to analyse or compare in detail the rival forces. Briefly, what was unhappily called the Invincible or Fortunate Armada consisted of some 130 ships, of which only about a third were warships, the remainder being armed transports for some 30,000 soldiers and cavalry.

Sidonia's flagship in the van was the *San Martin*. As the heart of the fleet, she was guarded on either side by four galleasses in case she was becalmed. Four war galleys also set out from Spain, but they never reached the Channel because they were unfit for navigation in the open sea. The old view that the Spanish ships were much larger and more heavily armed than the English is quite untenable. On average they were probably higher out of the water (which made them less manageable) and they were certainly more impressive to look at, with their sails emblazoned with coats of arms and religious symbols, but the odds were all in favour of the English, as neutral observers were well aware. In addition to the latter's proximity to base (a matter of the utmost importance in days when victuals would not last long), their superior seamanship and gunnery, and above all their high morale impressed such foreigners as the Venetian Ambassador. The English, he reported, 'never yield, and though driven back and thrown into confusion, they always return to the fight, thirsting for vengeance as long as they have a breath of life. In the present case they would consider themselves victorious, even if they died to a man along with the enemy, provided they could save the kingdom.' Even the Pope expressed his admiration after the Cadiz raid, though the Armada sailed with his blessing: 'Were the Queen only a Catholic she would be our best beloved daughter. Just look at Drake! Who is he? What forces has he? And yet he burned twenty-five of the King's ships.'

None the less it was a formidable fleet which the richest country in Europe sent to sea. To keep that mass of shipping together was a task in itself. To his credit, Sidonia performed it very successfully. His business was to reach Parma, not seek a fight. A tight formation protecting the transports was essential. According to English pictures of the event that formation was shaped like a crescent, with Sidonia in the centre. But this idea would never have been held if an aerial view had been possible. The formation adopted was almost certainly something in the shape of an eagle, with the flagship forming the head, two squadrons of warships on either side forming the wings, the large body of transports in the centre being protected in the rear by smaller squadrons of fighting ships. Seen from the rear (as the English saw them in the week-long chase up Channel), such a formation would naturally appear as a crescent or half-moon.

Nor were Spanish tactics as out of date as is commonly supposed. Santa Cruz, who had been in charge of the earlier plans, knew by experience that the future lay with the gun firing at long range (though extreme range was under a mile in those days) and not, as hitherto, by boarding. Broadsides, in fact, not broadswords would be the deciding factor. The King understood this perfectly well, but since the advantage of his ships lay in their height out of the water compared with the new type of Elizabethan galleon, he warned Sidonia what to expect: 'You should take special note that the enemy's aim will be to fight from a distance, since he has the advantage of superior artillery, while ours must be to attack and come to grips with the enemy at close quarters. . . . God granting victory, as a prudent commander, you should see that your squadrons do not break their battle formation, and that their commanders, moved by greed, do not give pursuit to the enemy and take prizes.'

Since we must follow the action from Drake's point of view, we should remember that Sidonia did as well as any man can have been expected to do in the circumstances. He held his fleet together; he refused to be deflected from his aim of taking the fleet up Channel without being involved in a general action; he reached Calais, if not Margate, with the loss of only two ships due to accidents and not enemy action. The defeat and destruction of the Armada came afterwards.

Although it was generally thought that Drake, in view of his reputation, would command the English fleet, this was not to be. Throughout that winter he was under the shadow of the Borough affair. It would have been madness to entrust the defence of England to a man whose behaviour towards his subordinate officers was so autocratic, especially as such officers were either older or equally cantankerous characters—Hawkins (now Treasurer of the Navy), or Frobisher (who always resented Drake's proud bearing). There was a good deal of distrust between Drake and the Navy Board, of which Borough was a member. It was more seemly, in view of Sidonia's appointment, to have at the head of affairs a nobleman who could keep the peace between such high-mettled subordinates. Lord Howard of Effingham (not a Catholic, as is sometimes said), the Lord Admiral of England, was the obvious choice. Like Sidonia, he had no experience at sea, but the office of Lord Admiral (the title of Lord High Admiral did not become common until the next century) had long been in his family, and it was fitting that the titular head of the Navy should fly the Royal Standard in the *Ark Royal*, a fine new galleon of 800 tons recently sold to the Crown by Sir Walter Raleigh, who had named her the *Ark Raleigh*. The appointment was made in December 1587, Drake being nominated his vice-admiral at Plymouth soon afterwards. What everyone wanted to know was how Drake would behave as a subordinate, and what his relationship with Howard would be when, in May 1588, the latter left Chatham (the main naval base) to bring the fleet round to Plymouth, leaving Lord Henry Seymour and Sir William Winter (Drake's companion on the first part of his voyage round the world) off the mouth of the Thames with fifty ships.

Most accounts of the campaign have been based, primarily, on a narrative written at Howard's orders by a Florentine resident in England named Petruccio Ubaldino. There is, however, another version commissioned from the same writer by Drake (who thought that the preceding narrative did scant justice to his part in the proceedings, which is true enough) has been translated and printed. It begins by showing how creditably Drake behaved when the Lord Admiral's ships were seen off Plymouth on May 23rd. Drake sailed out to meet him with his thirty ships in three lines ahead 'making a brave show of his skill and diligence'. Salutes were fired, drums and trumpets sounded, and the crews cheered. 'Sir Francis Drake, out of respect to the rank and dignity of the office and in honour of the Lord Admiral, lowered his own admiral's flag to pay tribute to Lord Howard, from whose ship the Vice-Admiral's flag was taken down and sent as a gift to Drake, who was thus able to use it as his own from that moment.' Thereafter all went well: to use Drake's words on another occasion, they were 'all of a company', since (says Ubaldino) he showed himself 'always of one mind and thought with the senior admiral, although there were those who had thought, or maybe feared, a different outcome'. That this is not a biased view is shown by a letter from Howard to Walsingham written a fortnight later in which he speaks appreciatively of 'how lovingly and kindly Sir Francis Drake beareth himself'. There can be little doubt that in the ensuing campaign Drake's advice was asked and taken very frequently by the Lord Admiral.

The fleet at Plymouth (excluding the fifty ships in the Downs) consisted of 102 ships, ranging in size from Frobisher's *Triumph* of 1,100 tons (the biggest Spanish ship was 1,249 tons) to the pinnaces used for scouting and maintaining contact with the shore. Many famous names in naval history can be found in the list—*Ark Royal*, *Lion*, *Tiger*, *Dreadnought*, *Victory* (Hawkins's flagship)—and nearly all the famous seamen of that great age were present, with the exception of Thomas Cavendish who was at that moment returning home after his successful repetition of Drake's circumnavigation of the world.

Drake himself flew his flag in the *Revenge*, rated as a ship of 500 tons, though we have seen that she was actually about 450. For this occasion she mounted 40 guns and was manned by a crew of 150 mariners, 24 gunners and 76 soldiers. She was one of Hawkins's new type of ship, heavily armed for her size, and extremely manœuvreable. She was one of the sixteen royal galleons, the other fifty-three belonging to private owners. They were equally well armed and showed much the same range of tonnage. In size there was, in fact, nothing to choose between the two fleets, though Howard had the inestimable advantage of not being encumbered with a body of transports. According to Spanish reports, the English fired three times as many shot as they did, but the 18 lb. and 9 lb. culverins and demi-culverins which formed their main armament were incapable of sinking wooden ships unless an explosion occurred. What they could and did do was to so batter, hull and dismast their opponents that the Spanish ships became uncontrollable in heavy weather.

It had been a difficult business keeping the ships in fighting trim that winter. As usual, the Queen blew hot and cold, sometimes ordering them to be laid up and their crews paid off, sometimes demanding that they should be fitted out with all expedition. Not the least of Drake's services was the way in which he kept the core of his fleet well manned and well victualled—largely at his own expense, though he was repaid his £9,000 later. Throughout the year it was not Elizabeth's parsimony which was at fault: the logistics (as we should call the business of arming and supplying the fleet) were far beyond the capacity of the Tudor administrative machine. Harassed officials and dishonest contractors were responsible for the shortages which undoubtedly occurred. Again and again Drake and Howard complain of the shortage of meat and beer. 'I know not,' runs one pathetic letter from Howard, 'which way to deal with the mariners to make them rest contented with sour beer.' But on the whole his letters are full of pride at the magnificent effort made by a nation so little prepared for war on this scale: 'I protest before God, and as my soul shall answer for it, that I think there never were in any place of the world worthier ships than these are, for so many. And as few we are, if the King of Spain's fleet be not hundreds, we will make good sport with them.' 'The gallantest company of captains, soldiers and mariners that I think ever were seen in England,' he told Burghley soon after he joined forces with Drake.

The relation between the two men was much the same as that between Sidonia and Valdes, though on a more cordial and candid footing. Drake's tactical and strategic advice was as sound as we should expect of him, but it was not in accordance with the Queen's more conservative views. In her opinion the function of the fleet was purely defensive. The ships, she said, must 'ply up and down' the chops of the Channel to intercept the Armada as it swung eastward out of the Bay of Biscay. She had no conception how broad the seas were, or how easy it was to miss a fleet, even if it was composed of a hundred and fifty sail.

Drake, on the other hand, persistently advocated offensive tactics. From his day to that of Nelson and up to the present the advice of all those who appreciate the flexibility of sea power has invariably been that the enemy coastline is the first line of defence. 'My very good Lords,' he wrote to the

Council, 'next under God's protection, the advantage and gain of time and place will be the only and chief means for our good; wherein I most humbly beseech your good Lordships to persevere as you have begun, for that with fifty sail of shipping we shall do more good upon their own coast than a great many more will do here at home.' The Lord Admiral was soon won over to this point of view, but the Queen would not approve until both Hawkins and Frobisher had lent their support to it. On 30th May, therefore, the fleet put to sea. Had they known it, the Armada left Lisbon only a few days earlier.

The battle which Drake hoped for never took place. The first of the gales of that stormy summer blew up, forcing the English back to Plymouth and the Spanish into Corunna. Twice again the English fleet sailed into the Bay, but they never saw an enemy ship. On the last occasion the same southerly wind which drove them back enabled the Spaniards to make their final departure from Corunna.

It was on Friday, July 19th (29th July by our calendar) that Captain Fleming of the *Golden Hind* (not Drake's ship) came scudding into Plymouth Sound before a strong westerly wind with the news that the enormous array of Spanish ships had been sighted off the Lizard. Everyone knows the story of how he found Drake and the other captains of the fleet playing bowls upon the Hoe where Drake's statue now stands. The English ships were huddled in harbour, the wind blowing directly on shore, the enemy a few miles out to sea. It was in such circumstances that Drake is supposed to have said, 'Play out the game: there's time for that and to beat the Spanish after'.

Since the story has become part of our national heritage, and since no contemporary chronicler mentions the incident, it is worth inquiring into its origins. That Drake and his companions were playing bowls is likely enough, though it is first mentioned in an obscure anti-Spanish propaganda pamphlet of fictional content entitled *Vox Populi* in 1624. That Drake must have realized the importance of getting to sea as quickly as possible, if they were to avoid being caught as he had caught the Spanish at Cadiz the previous summer, is surely obvious. Hence that he should have made the remarks attributed to him is in the highest degree unlikely. In fact it is not until 1736 that any such story is told. In a life of Raleigh published that year the author, a certain William Oldys, refers to the bowls story and adds, 'the tradition goes that Drake would needs see the game up, but was soon prevailed on to go and play out the rubbers with the Spaniards.' From such doubtful origins has one of our best-known legends arisen.

That the English escaped from a highly dangerous situation is due to two things—their magnificent seamanship, which enabled them to beat out of the Sound against the wind; and the fact that Sidonia allowed them time to do so (though Howard reports that they did it 'very hardly'), because he had to heave to off Falmouth on Saturday to enable his fleet to regroup after their rough passage through the Bay. Meanwhile the alarm had been given inland. Beacons were lit 'From Eddystone to Berwick bounds, from Lynn to Milford Bay,' according to Macaulay's ballad. How the southern counties of England were roused is shown by this sort of entry in the parish accounts of Launceston, near Drake's birthplace: 'Paid to Jasper Bedlime to warn the parish that they should be ready at an hour's warning, 11d.'

By the Sunday morning the two fleets were in the positions which they were to retain for the next week, the English in no particular order lying astern and to windward of the slowly moving formation of the Armada ('all the world never saw such a force as theirs was,' reported Howard). The way he had obtained the weather gauge must have surprised and annoyed the enemy. During the previous night he had led most of his fleet across the front of their formation, tacking past the Eddystone rock to take up a position astern of them and join up with those ships which had worked their way along the coast from Plymouth.

We have no certain knowledge of the tactics of the English as they proceeded to harry the rear of the Spanish fleet. They were certainly not the strict line-ahead formation which later imposed a formal pattern upon naval warfare. Probably they were something in the nature of 'follow-my-leader', with groups of ships standing in to deliver a broadside and then sheering off again to rejoin the main body. Howard was later criticised for not coming to grips with the enemy, but in view of their tight formation there can be no doubt that he acted correctly, though it was not till he was off the Isle of Wight that he formed his own fleet into four distinct divisions under himself, Hawkins, Frobisher and Drake.

Night stations were a more difficult matter at a date when recognition signals had not been invented. As the fleet passed Bolt Head on the Sunday night Drake was told to 'set the watch' by lighting the lantern on his poop, which the rest of the ships would follow. Inasmuch as he was given the post of honour to lead the fleet, what happened that night between Start Point and Berry Head seems all the more reprehensible to us, though there is no contemporary criticism of his action beyond a jealous remark made by Frobisher who, speaking of the prize Drake was to capture, swore that 'he thinketh to cozen us of our shares of 15,000 ducats, but we will have our shares, or I will make him spend the best blood in his belly'.

What happened was this: in the middle of the night Drake's light vanished from the sight of those who were following him, which naturally created a certain amount of disorder in the fleet. Drake says that he left his post in order to examine some strange sail which were passing on the opposite tack, and certainly there were a few neutral vessels in the vicinity at the time. By so doing he caught sight of a galleon looming up ahead, her bowsprit and foremast gone, obviously in distress, and obviously separated from the rest of the Armada. She was the *Nuestra Señora del Rosario*, flagship of the Biscayan squadron, whose captain, Don Pedro de Valdes, was the best seaman in the fleet. He had had the misfortune to come into collison with another ship the previous evening and he could not catch up with the rest of the fleet again. Now, summoned to surrender just before dawn and knowing that his opponent was the redoubtable Drake, Valdes gave in without a blow. Needless to say, he was treated with Drake's customary courtesy on board the *Revenge*, eating at his table and sharing his cabin throughout the ensuing action. Drake's humanity is in strong contrast with the behaviour of the officials at Dartmouth, whither the prize was sent, who declared it was a pity her crew had not been pitched overboard. There is a tradition that the gallery of Dartmouth church is constructed out of the timbers of the *Rosario*. True or not, she was the only prize taken during the campaign, apart from the wreck of the *San Salvador*, which was towed into Weymouth after an internal explosion. Of course Drake benefited by his prisoner's ransom, which amounted to £3,000.

On the Monday morning he rejoined the fleet off Berry Head. There was a possibility that Sidonia might do what William III did in the only successful invasion of Britain a hundred years later—land in Torbay. But he never seems to have entertained the idea, sailing slowly on up Channel at an average speed of only two knots.

Off Portland Bill the wind dropped. A sharp action ensued in which Frobisher's inshore squadron was hard pressed by the Spaniards, who saw a chance of cutting it off from the rest of Howard's fleet. So confused are the accounts of what happened that we can only say the attack was called off when Drake threatened to destroy their formation on the right. Much the same thing happened in the equally confusing action off the Isle of Wight the next day. This time it was Hawkins who took the initiative by attempting to cut off an isolated galleon. The curious part about this affair was that for once oars supplanted sail power. The weather being calm, both Hawkins and Howard had themselves towed into action by row boats, but the Spanish galleasses (designed for this sort of occasion) proved singularly ineffective.

As the weather continued calm on Friday the Lord Admiral took the opportunity of exercising his prerogative to confer the honour of knighthood on his captains, Hawkins of the *Victory*, Frobisher of the *Triumph*, Beeston of the *Dreadnought* and others. Drake, we may presume, attended the ceremony on board the *Ark Royal* to watch the proceedings with a benevolent eye.

On Saturday evening, the wind freshening a little, the Armada came to anchor off Calais. Margate, as Philip intended, was out of the question now that Seymour with his fifty ships joined Howard, bringing the English total to one hundred and forty ships. At Calais Sidonia imagined that it would be possible to get in touch with Parma, but he reckoned without the wind and tide of Sunday night. Howard realized how important it was that he should be driven from his anchorage before the Spanish army leaders knew that he had arrived, so all that day, under the superintendence of Captains Yonge and Prouse, eight fireships had been secretly prepared. The tide served at midnight. Having fixed their sails and primed the guns, the crews climbed over the side into boats towing alongside, leaving the fireships to drift slowly down upon the compact body of the Spanish fleet.

In a moment all was confusion. Three years previously when Parma was at Antwerp, the Dutch had blown up a bridge of boats with some devilish contrivance of floating mines. Many on board the Spanish galleons expected the same thing to happen now, as they saw bearing down upon them these vessels 'spurting fire and their ordnance shooting, which was a horror to see in the night'.

There is an old saying that ships fear fire more than water. It was certainly true at a date when wooden hulls, the seams payed with tar, cordage, canvas and open buckets of gunpowder below decks made them highly inflammable. No wonder that on this occasion panic broke out in the Spanish fleet. Every ship fended for herself. Cables were cut and anchors lost. Hulls and rigging were damaged as the disorderly mass struggled out to what they hoped was the safety of the open sea. Some ran ashore, notably the huge galleasse *San Lorenzo*, which drifted on to Calais bar.

Dawn on Monday saw a collection of ships strung out along the Banks of Zeeland between Gravelines and Dunkirk. It was now that Elizabeth's policy of assisting the Dutch rebels paid a dividend. From their base at Flushing the Sea Devils effectively blocked any passage up to Antwerp, which was still in Spanish hands. The situation in which the Spanish fleet found itself was a sailor's nightmare. Their retreat was cut off, a north-westerly wind was driving them on to a lee shore on a shelving coast, their ships were leaking from the various shot holes received in the bombardments in the Channel, their water and food was almost gone, since they had been at sea nearly three weeks and the fireship attack prevented them from replenishing their supplies at Calais; above all, they had lost their anchors when they cut their cables on that fatal night.

It is at this point of the campaign that Drake steps into the limelight as the real admiral of England. If his behaviour in snapping up the *Rosario* is open to criticism, how much more so is that of Howard when he yielded to the temptation of rifling the stranded *San Lorenzo* at the mouth of Calais harbour. Drake now seized the initiative to sail into the attack which opened the battle of Gravelines. The *Revenge*, closely followed by other ships (including Howard's), swept up to pour in a broadside at close range at the *San Martin*. Then, hauling into the wind, she came round again to deliver another shattering blow.

So it went on for eight hours, the English ships firing whenever they could get close enough, and the Spaniards striving for sea room as they returned the fire. Misinterpreting Drake's tactics, Frobisher after the battle accused him—of all things—of cowardice: 'He came bragging up at the first, indeed, and gave them his prow and his broadside; and then kept his luff and was glad he was gone again like a cowardly knave.' From Ubaldino's narrative we have a clearer idea what it was like on board the *Revenge*: 'His cabin was twice pierced by cannon balls and there was an occasion on which two gentlemen, who towards evening had retired to rest a little, and one of them lying upon the bed, when it was broken under him by a saker ball, without his taking the least hurt. And shortly afterwards the Earl of Northumberland, who had come to fight as a volunteer, and Sir Charles Blount, were resting on the same bed in the same place when it was again hit by a ball of a demi-culverin which passed through the cabin from one side to another without doing any harm than scrape the foot, taking off the toes of one who was there with them.'

On Tuesday morning a miracle—so it seemed to the Spaniards—occurred. The wind shifted from west-north-west to west-south-west, enabling the Armada to steer for the open sea, leaving behind them half a dozen wrecks on the Banks of Zeeland. Drake was well pleased with the result, for now any junction with Parma was out of the question, and we have seen how he always feared Parma's army rather than Sidonia's fleet. 'We have them before us', he wrote in a hurried note to Walsingham as he set course in pursuit to the northward, 'and mind with the grace of God to wrestle a pull with him. There was never anything pleased me better than seeing the enemy flying with a southerly wind to the northwards. God grant you have a good eye to the Duke of Parma, for with the grace of God, if we live, I doubt not but ere it will be long so to handle the matter with the Duke of Sidonia as he shall wish himself at St. Mary Port [his home near Cadiz] among his orange trees.'

By the time they were off Newcastle, Howard and Drake decided to give up the pursuit. The expenditure of ammunition had been unprecedented. The fleet had been at sea without watering for ten days. Victuallers and supply ships had done their part, running out of all the southern harbours to join the ships as they came up Channel, but now the chase was so swift they could not catch up with the fleet, and the warships were entering the territorial waters of Scotland, at that time a foreign power. Disease—typhus, dysentery and scurvy—was breaking out among the crews (though it is significant that Drake's ship does not seem to have suffered in this way), so that it was vital to return to the mouth of the Thames as quickly as possible, in order to discharge the men.

Well satisfied with their work in chasing the Spanish fleet away from their coasts, the admirals returned to London, leaving the enemy to stagger on northabout round Scotland to their fate. Scouts followed them as far north as the Orkneys, but when the Armada turned into the teeth of the westerly gale which was now blowing up, they left it, knowing for sure that its destruction was inevitable. During the following weeks news filtered into the Court at London of galleons wrecked upon the Outer Hebrides, or driven ashore upon the rocky coasts of Donegal, Connaught and Galway. A few Spanish officers made their escape across Ireland by reason of their religion and their money, but most of the crews were butchered by the savage Irish as they waded ashore from their shipwrecked vessels. Encouraged by fantastic stories of Spanish iniquity which the English garrison commanders took pains to spread, the Irish peasants and the English soldiery showed little mercy. Some twenty-five galleons perished in this way, the total losses being sixty-four ships and about ten thousand men. One galleon, indeed, was driven so far east that she was wrecked off Bolt Head in Devonshire. Today, with the development of underwater archaeology, these wrecks, and the treasure of the Armada which lies beneath the waves, are attracting the attention of divers. The most successful excavation has been that of the galleasse *Gerona* which ran on the rocks near the Giant's Causeway. Gold, jewels, silver chains, nautical instruments, bronze cannon, 405 gold coins and 756 of silver were recovered from the seabed and are now housed in a special museum at Belfast.

Our last picture of Sidonia before he reached refuge in the port of Santander in northern Spain on 11th September is of a man sitting in his cabin, his head in his hands, his hair grey with anxiety under the disaster which had overtaken him. 'The troubles and miseries we have suffered cannot be described to your Majesty,' he wrote, 'they have been greater than I have ever been seen in any voyage before.' As he journeyed overland to his orange groves near Cadiz the crowds in the towns which he passed through jeered at him with shouts of, 'Here comes Drake!'

To commemorate the victory a medal was struck on which were inscribed the words *Flavit Jehovah et Dissipati Sunt*. Similarly at a thanksgiving service held at St. Paul's Cathedral on November 24th there was 'a song made by her Majesty and sung before her at her coming from Whitehall to Paul's through Fleet Street after the scattering of the Spanish Navy', in which the Queen thanked God who:

> Made the winds and waters rise
> To scatter all mine enemies.

Drake, who presumably attended the service, may well have thought that some credit might also be given to those who, at the battle of Gravelines, had won the first great victory in British naval history.

CHAPTER NINE

*

The Lisbon Expedition

The fortunes of Drake's career trace a curve which rises with a brilliant, almost uninterrupted record of success for twenty years until it reaches a climax at the battle of Gravelines, after which it declines during the last eight years of his life into a story of failure and disgrace, which is only partially redeemed by the events of his last voyage. There are those, of course, for whom Drake can do no wrong. Such uncritical hero worshippers are not content with the way in which a penniless freebooter rose to be the first great admiral in British history.

The lives of Drake and Nelson have, indeed, become part of our national heritage, but it is futile to make comparisons between them, so different are the circumstances of their lives and the problems which confronted them.

Even if Drake is not so great an admiral as Nelson, or so fine an explorer as Cook, as a fighting seaman he is pre-eminent. Unless we are bemused with the legends which have grown up about his name, we must recognize and allow for his shortcomings. He was not trained as an administrator or a statesman, so that when he left the realm of tactics for those of logistics or administration his shortcomings become obvious. In command of a squadron with the enemy in sight, there has been no one in history to equal him. In command of a fleet, with diplomatic or financial responsibilities to consider, he was not so successful. His rough, independent character made him a difficult man to co-operate with, and the course of his life left him ignorant of the political stakes involved in matters of grand strategy. He saw things in black and white: Spain was antichrist, her treasure his legitimate loot. The Queen, however, unversed as she may have been in the art of war, was supremely success-ful in the more difficult art of the statesman who had to weigh the resources of her small kingdom against those of the world-wide empire of Spain. If Philip II had produced an admiral of the stature of Drake, the history of the British Isles would have taken a less happy course, because Spain had the best army and potentially the best navy in sixteenth-century Europe.

After the defeat of the Armada It was naturally on Drake's advice that Elizabeth leaned. If the line of action adopted can be shown to be his and not hers, we must apportion the blame justly. It has been usual to make her responsible for the failure of the Lisbon expedition of 1589, but the more that is known about this 'miserable action' (as one of Drake's companions called it) the more obvious does it become that it was the admiral and even more the general— Sir John Norris (or Norreys)—and not Burghley's timidity or the Queen's habitual parsimony which were responsible for the outcome.

To what extent was it possible in the autumn of 1588 to estimate the damage done to the Spanish Armada? The immediate threat of invasion had obviously been dispelled. Unverified reports of wrecks along the western coasts kept coming in. There was also substantial news that fifty ships had returned to Santander and other ports of northern Spain under Sidonia's leadership. In spite of his tendency to brag, Drake never claimed that the Armada had been destroyed. 'If I have not performed as much as was looked for,' he wrote with unusual humility, 'yet I persuade myself his good Lordship (Burghley) will confess I have been dutiful.'

In public, however, a pamphlet appeared which may well have been inspired by him. Its aim was to deny Spanish claims that the events of that summer were not a very serious matter after all. It has a typical sixteenth-century title, the merit of which (unlike so many titles of our own day) was to give a full idea of the contents of the book: *A Pack of Spanish Lies sent abroad into the world, translated out of the original and now ripp'd up, unfolded, and by just examination condemned, as containing false, corrupt and detestable wares, worthy to be damn'd and burnt*. 'With all their great terrible ostentation,' says the author, 'they did not in all their sailing about England, so much as sink or take one ship, bark, pinnace or cockboat of ours, or even burn so much as a sheepcote on this land.'

True enough. But what about the fifty sail which had returned home, most of them warships? It was obvious that the English victory must be followed up. Never was there a better opportunity of striking Philip a mortal blow. Two-thirds of his fleet had been destroyed, his army in the Low Countries was locked up, his credit in the eyes of European bankers stood very low. In September Drake found it easy to persuade the Queen that she could muster a fleet little inferior in size to that of the Armada itself, and immensely superior in composition and leadership. It would not be burdened with vast numbers of transports, though it would carry a high proportion of soldiers, and it would be led by a man whose very name—El Draque, the Dragon—struck terror to the Spaniards, and by a general, Sir John Norris, who had seen long service in the religious wars in France, the rebellion in the Low Countries, and the suppression of discontent in Ireland, where Drake first made his acquaintance before the voyage round the world. Unfortunately 'Black John' Norris was one of those professional soldiers of fortune who knew nothing about military affairs except how to fight: his advice was consistently bad, and the business of supplying the great force now put under his control was quite beyond him.

For reasons which it is difficult to fathom, army ideas prevailed in the organization of the fleet, though this was no great fault if we recall what excellent results were obtained by Cromwell's Generals-at-Sea fifty years later. Perhaps the lack of organization on the English side compared with that of the Spaniards during the late campaign had been noted; at all events, naval organization was something new at that date, whereas the military side of war was already something of a science. In the expedition now contemplated the troops were divided into companies and regiments (a new feature in English history), and the six squadrons of ships were commanded by 'colonels', even the pinnaces being under a Master of Discoveries, or Intelligence Officer, as we should call him.

To raise the force Drake and Norris had in mind they were given leave to conscript six thousand men in this country, to be supplemented by another 3,500 to be withdrawn from the English troops stationed in the Low Countries. One of the chief reasons for the fatal delay in the sailing of the expedition was the fact that the Dutch and even the English commanders there justifiably resented this breach of the Queen's promise to keep her troops in that part of Europe. Nor did the former regard the demand that they should produce transports, sailors and ammunition with a favourable eye. As for the troops raised at home, all agreed that they were 'loose, disordered persons . . . the scum and dregs of this country'.

Another mistake was made when the Queen adopted the old idea of making this another of those joint-stock operations which had been so successful in the past. The method had certainly worked well before, but the stage for that sort of amateur warfare was now over. She therefore agreed to Drake's proposal that she should provide six royal ships, siege guns, £20,000 in cash and payment for three months' victuals. For his part he and Norris promised to put up another £20,000 each, and to raise twenty more ships from private hands; hence the list of ships engaged contains such names as the *Emmanuel* of Dartmouth, *Mayflower* of Yarmouth, *Minion* of Fowey, *Toby* of Harwich, *William* of Ipswich, etc.

When Drake's 'armada' (as we may call it on account of its size) sailed in April 1589 the number of ships had risen to eighty and the troops amounted to about twenty thou- to one hundred and fifty, mostly small vessels of under 200 tons. The troops amounted to about twenty thousand, though it is typical of the inefficient organization that Dutch were proving difficult, Drake had no hesitation in seizing sixty of their 'fly boats' which he met by chance in the Channel on his way down to Plymouth. Of these, twenty-five deserted at the first opportunity, their crews having 'carried themselves very frowardly', as might be expected under the circumstances.

Nor is it surprising that the victualling organization broke down before the start. An extraordinary letter from Norris to Burghley blackmailed the Lord Treasurer into providing another £4,000 by threatening to turn this horde of Falstaffs, Bardolphs and Pistols loose upon the countryside if payment were not forthcoming: 'If the wind continues against us, we are utterly unable to supply ourselves, and, the voyage breaking (i.e. failing), we cannot think what to do with the army.' As a matter of fact when all was over this is precisely what did happen: bands of demobilized soldiers wandered about the southern counties to swell the numbers of rogues and vagabonds, 'the caterpillars of the commonwealth', which formed a permanent social problem in Elizabethan England. Neither of the leaders seems to have realized that, even if Parliament agreed to their plans and voted the necessary monies, the business of levying taxes was slow and uncertain, Elizabethans being (as might be expected) past masters in the arts of tax evasion.

It was, of course, the six months' delay in the launching of the expedition which led to this state of affairs. Planned for September, the sailing date was postponed by the dilatoriness of the Dutch to February, and then further delayed until April on account of the seasonal south-westerly gales. Even then the force sailed without siege artillery, apart from more serious deficiencies in food, drink and even small arms. By April £96,000 had been spent, whereas £70,000 was budgeted for. No wonder the Queen began to doubt the wisdom of leaving it all to her commanders.

The objectives of the expedition were clearly laid down by the Queen. First, the destruction of the remnant of the Armada in the ports between Santander on the east and Corunna on the west. Secondly, the capture of Lisbon, if, as the sponsors assured her, there was a Portuguese uprising to welcome Dom Antonio the Pretender when they landed Third, an attack on the Azores with the aim of making those islands a base from which it would be possible to intercept the returning treasure fleets of Spain. Again and again Elizabethan strategy returned to this last point as the surest way of robbing the King of Spain of the means of continuing the war. Again and again the base failed to materialize.

This time, at any rate, Drake's orders were not ambiguous: 'Before you shall attempt either Portugal or the Azores our express pleasure and commandment is that you distress the ships of war in Guipuzcoa, Biscay and Galicia, that they may not impeach you in such enterprises as you they may do us no harm in your absence.' This, in the Queen's view, was exactly what Drake and Norris failed to do.

From the political point of view Drake pinned his faith in Dom Antonio, the pretender to the Portuguese throne. Ever since 1581, when Drake first plotted with him, this pathetic and ineffective figure had been trailing from place to place, selling his jewels to support himself when not enjoying Drake's hospitality at Buckland Abbey. The Tudor age was similar to our own in the techniques adopted to promote discontent in hostile countries—plotting the overthrow or assassination of foreign princes, sending 'volunteers' to assist rebellious subjects. Thus Philip plotted to have Elizabeth killed in order to replace her by Mary, Queen of Scots; he sympathized with the Irish rebels, and actively assisted the Catholic League in the Wars of Religion in France. For her part, Elizabeth backed the Huguenots, sent 'volunteers' to the Low Countries to assist the Dutch rebels, and harboured the exiled Dom Antonio. Unfortunately the latter was quite out of touch with his native country, so that when Drake landed him in Portugal there were no signs of a 'resistance' movement to welcome him.

The expedition sailed on 8th April, 1589, Drake's flagship being once more the *Revenge*, of which his younger brother Thomas was now captain. At the last moment a most unfortunate incident occurred. Drake was in no way to blame, but it proved the last straw for the Queen. The hotheaded young Earl of Essex, her special favourite, decided (like Sir Philip Sidney on a previous occasion) to run away from Court to seek honour and fame on the beaches of Portugal. It must have been a last-minute decision, for the Earl rode the two hundred and thirty miles to Plymouth in forty-eight hours to get there in time. Elizabeth was furious. High-ranking officials were sent posting down to Plymouth to bring him back. Drake denied all knowledge of his whereabouts, but several of his ships had already sailed, among them the *Swiftsure* commanded by an old Welsh soldier, Sir Roger Williams, and it was in her that the errant Earl had hidden himself. The messengers returned disconsolate to London, whereupon the Queen composed a blistering letter to the commanders of the expedition, which they received two months later off the coast of Portugal. Sir Roger was the chief object of her wrath—'his offence is in so high a degree that the same deserveth to be punished by death, which if you have not already done, then we will and command you that you sequester him from all charge and service, and cause him to be safely kept, until you shall know our further pleasure therein, as you will answer for the contrary at your perils.' As for Essex, 'we straightly charge you that you do forthwith cause him to be sent hither in safe manner. Which if you do not, you shall look to answer for the same to your smart, for these be no childish actions. Therefore consider well of your doing herein.' With the Queen in that mood there was bound to be trouble when they returned, as they did, with other misdoings to report.

On April 24th the fleet was off Corunna—not Santander. Drake claimed that he had received reports of a concentration of shipping there. He found one large galleon and a few small vessels, whereas there were forty galleons at Santander.

The town of Corunna is built in two parts, a higher well-fortified citadel, and a lower commercial city. In his usual way Drake went straight in to the attack, hoping to seize the neck of the peninsula on which the lower town was built in much the same way as he had taken Cartagena by storm. Seven thousand men were landed in three hours (a remarkable feat, if true), one body being commanded by the same Captain Sampson who had led the 'forlorn' along the beach at low water at Cartagena. This time the water was too deep. The city wall had to be scaled. After bitter fighting Norris took possession of the lower town, while the Spaniards retreated to the safety of the upper town on the rocky tip of the peninsula. While the rabble which composed most of his army looted the shops and taverns, Norris led the better-disciplined troops to attack the citadel of the upper town. For a fortnight they made little progress. Even when an elaborate mine was sprung under the battlements, half of the tower fell down on the heads of the attackers.

Meanwhile the Spaniards themselves had burned the galleon in the harbour, and a prisoner reported that a large force was gathering in a neighbouring village to drive the English into the sea. Norris's brother (an equally tough professional soldier, easily recognizable by a scar on his forehead which a drunken Dutchman had given him with the lid of a tankard) was sent to drive them off. Pike in hand, he led his men across a narrow bridge at the end of which he thrust at a Spanish soldier so violently that he overreached himself and received a sword cut in his leg. Seeing the danger he was in, his brother snatched up another pike and dashed to his support. His example fired the men behind him, who rushed the bridge and overran the camp beyond it. The enemy were mostly peasants who knew the countryside too well to be followed. They scattered along the same road by the side of which Sir John Moore was killed in the famous retreat to Corunna in 1809.

It was a victory, but not a brilliant one. There was nothing more to be done at Corunna. Indeed it was vitally important to get the troops out of the town as soon as possible. Wine barrels, not cannon shot, had almost destroyed the army. Having sailed short of food and drink, the men were starving for plunder. The lice-carried disease of typhus had already begun to take its toll. Intoxication on a grand scale did the rest. Thenceforward men died by hundreds daily, so that within three months Drake's force was reduced by ten thousand men without any serious fighting having taken place.

In view of the Queen's orders, why did he proceed south to Lisbon and not east to Santander? In his despatches he seems to have forgotten the existence of the latter place. Only later, when he was charged with disobeying the first article of his instructions, did he find an excuse in a contrary wind and a dangerous shore. The fact that he wrote demanding the siege artillery which had been promised him suggests that Dom Antonio's scheme of attacking Lisbon had now taken precedence in his mind over the Queen's orders.

To attack the capital city of Portugal without siege artillery he decided to do on a larger scale what he had done so well at Santo Domingo—use the army in a flank attack, while he took the fleet up the Tagus for a frontal attack. So Norris, Dom Antonio and the army were landed at a small place named Peniche about fifty miles north of Lisbon. The landing was successful, Essex earning high praise for bravery, even though there was little opposition. The long march to Lisbon was also unopposed; but Norris arrived before the walls of one of the biggest cities in Europe without the means to attack it, without allies to assist him, or even a fleet to give covering fire. His troops, decimated by disease, were totally exhausted after their long march through a parched countryside in the height of summer without any wheeled transport for their baggage. Nor was there any sign of any enthusiasm for the cause of the Pretender.

Meanwhile, only twelve miles distant from the city, the fleet remained at anchor at the mouth of the river. The reason for this strange inactivity on Drake's part seems to have been partly contrary winds and partly, it must be supposed, Drake's loss of nerve. Perhaps his faith in himself had been shaken by the post-mortem on the Borough affair. He simply could not take the risks of another quarrel with the Lord Treasurer, nor of having the only means of retreat destroyed by the powerful forts guarding the river, though he reduced one of these without much difficulty and it is clear that scurvy was now widespread: 'The sickness and weakness of the mariners and soldiers was so extreme as they were not able to handle the tackle of the ships.' After all was over it was Drake, not Norris, who was blamed.

Days passed, and still no word came from Norris. At last, just as the admiral was preparing to move, messengers arrived to tell him that the army was in full retreat. Led by a resolute general with the unusual title of Cardinal-Archduke (he was Philip's nephew), the local levies had thrust Norris's men from the outer suburbs and were hustling them back to the protection of their ships. Once out of touch with the enemy, their courage revived. Norris sent a futile challenge to the Cardinal-Archduke offering to fight a pitched battle the next day. The romantic Essex went one better by offering to fight the best man the Spaniards could put up either hand to hand or in a medieval tourney of six a side. When Norris marched forward the next day the Spaniards, having done what they wanted to do, had of course disappeared.

At the councils of war held on board the *Revenge* there were heated arguments as to what to do next, each service blaming the other for what had already happened. It was dangerous to hang about much longer, because the ships they had failed to destroy in the north might make their appearance. No victuallers or guns arrived from England, only the violent letter from the Queen about Essex. Typhus and dysentery were killing off the troops at a deadly rate. Fortunately a collection of unarmed cargo ships, sixty neutral Hanseatic vessels loaded with grain for Philip's fleet, happened to appear to seaward, having sailed from the Baltic northabout round Scotland without knowing that Drake was lying off the mouth of the Tagus. They were soon 'fetched in' on the legitimate excuse that they were carrying contraband to the enemy. Such were the only prizes taken during this expedition. Instead of another treasure ship like the *San Felipe*, all that Drake could offer for sale on his return were a few brass guns, the cargoes of grain having been consumed by his starving crews.

To redeem matters the English commanders talked of stretching across to the Azores. But again contrary winds prevented them, and a serious leak which developed in the *Revenge* forced them to change their plans. On their way northward Vigo was sacked for the second time in Drake's career, but nothing worth taking was found in the town, and it is a sad commentary on the state of his force that only 2,000 men out of the original 20,000 were fit enough to land. There was nothing for it but to return home, which they did at the end of June.

Casualty estimates vary between eight and ten thousand men dead, not of wounds, but of drink and disease. One galleon had been burned by the Spaniards. Dom Antonio's cause was totally discredited, and so was the leadership of Norris and Drake. The latter's original intention of not just singeing the King of Spain's beard, but of lighting 'a fire in the King of Spain's own house', had failed entirely. A great opportunity had been missed. By next year Philip had recovered sufficiently to begin building a new Armada, one of the features of which was the introduction of the new *fregatas* or fast-sailing galleons, from which we derive the word 'frigate'. The assassination of Henry III gave him the opportunity of interfering more boldly on the Catholic side in France, and his warships enabled him to make landings —fortunately unimportant in their results—in Brittany and southern Ireland. Instead of £20,000, Elizabeth had paid out £50,000, apart from losing a high proportion of her regular army on a task which had not even been attempted. For the next seven years she was condemned to play a defensive role, because, as she complained, her commanders had gone 'to places more for profit than for service'.

An apologist who served under Drake summarized the achievements of that summer in the following words—'In this short time of our adventure we have won a town by escalade, battered and assaulted another, overthrown a mighty prince's power in the field, landed an army in three several places in his kingdom, marched seven days in the heart of his country, lain three nights in the suburbs of his principal city, beaten his forces into the gates thereof, and possessed two of his frontier forts.'

To Elizabeth, however, the failure merited a court martial on the leaders. Like Oliver Cromwell, she was a hard task-master when things went wrong. The 'articles of accusation' which she brought against Norris and Drake included failure to destroy the Spanish warships, wasting time attacking the wrong place, landing in Portugal without making sure that the country would rise in their support. They had spent a great deal more money than she could afford, and they had harboured Essex against her express wishes. It was a formidable bill of indictment. Had she been like her father, Drake and Norris would have lost their heads,

CHAPTER TEN

*

The Last Voyage

After the failure of the Lisbon Expedition Drake did not go to sea again for six years. In the Queen's eyes he was in disgrace, and it was particularly unfortunate for him that his two most powerful friends at Court—Leicester and Walsingham—died about this time. For advice on how to prosecute the naval war Elizabeth turned to her older commander, Sir John Hawkins, who, as Treasurer of the Navy Board for the past twelve years, had built for her the most efficient navy in Europe. The tragedy of the next stage of the war was that this magnificent instrument was not used by a Queen who was better versed in political than in naval strategy.

Hawkins's advice was to establish a regular blockade of Spain based on the Azores. He contemplated sending out a sequence of squadrons composed of five or six of the latest type of galleon to cruise between the Azores and the Spanish mainland for a few months at a time. Since everyone was agreed that the chief naval objective was to intercept the returning fully laden treasure fleets on which Philip's ability to continue the war depended, Hawkins's plan had the virtue of a systematic attempt to ensure this, instead of the occasional summer cruises favoured by more amateur leaders. Unfortunately the latter course was the one adopted, because, as Raleigh complained, 'Her Majesty did all things

by halves, and by petty invasions taught the Spaniard h
to defend himself.'

In later centuries blockade by naval forces became
linchpin of naval strategy, but the method was far beyo
the means of Elizabethan sea power. Hawkins's plan
never tried out as he intended because an operational b
in the Azores never became available, nor could the ship
his day keep the seas for long enough periods to maintai
serious watch because both their victualling and th
maintenance were still woefully inadequate. Sour beer,
meat and the depredations of *teredo navalis*—the naval wo
which bored holes in the bottoms of wooden ships—w
more serious enemies than all the galleons of Spain. N
could Hawkins, when he originated the idea of a strate
blockade, realize the number of relief ships necessary
maintain a constant force on station, as in the days
Nelson.

Instead of the Azores blockade there was a series of
effective summer cruises on the part of individuals
Frobisher, Lord Thomas Howard, Sir Richard Grenv
and the Earl of Cumberland (Drake's most distinguis
imitator in the art of raiding the West Indies). The only
of these cruises which has achieved immortality was that
1591, when Grenville's last fight of the *Revenge* resulted
the loss of one of the only two warships to be lost to Sp
during the whole course of the war. It must have b
peculiarly galling to Drake at home at Plymouth to see, f
Frobisher (his rival in popular esteem) sail in his old f
ship, and then Grenville (his private enemy) lose the s
albeit in a heroic fight.

It was not only the shortcomings of Hawkins's navy t
were responsible for the failure of his plan. As we have s
Philip of Spain virtually rebuilt his fleet during those ye
A regular convoy system for the treasure fleets was in

tuted, in which his new *fregatas* of the Indian Guard provided protection for the smaller, faster vessels called *gallezabras* in which the treasure was shipped. Over the most dangerous part of the voyage, that is between the Azores and the mainland, fleets from Spanish and Portuguese ports put out to bring the *flotas* safely home to Lisbon or Seville. It was one such fleet which caught Grenville at Flores. The English had their successes—Cumberland's capture of a town in the Azores, which ought to have been turned into a base, or the capture of the *Madre de Dios* by Captain Cross, the richest prize of the war—but on the whole the strategy failed to defeat Spain by naval means.

During the six years of his retirement from the sea we must not imagine that such an active personality as Drake's was idle. He did not, like Achilles, sulk in his tent. From his home at Buckland Abbey he carried out the duties of Mayor of Plymouth, and from his London house in Dowgate Ward he was an active member of Parliament. He sat on various committees, such as that on Liberties and Privileges, and (oddly enough) that on Ecclesiastical Court Bills. Among such committees we may be sure that none interested him more than that for relieving sick and wounded soldiers and sailors. In 1590 he and Hawkins founded a most important naval charity for this purpose—the Chatham Chest. This was a huge iron box with a small hole in the lid through which seamen put sixpence a month out of their pay as a contributory pension scheme. The funds of the Chest (which is really the first of welfare state schemes) were later transferred to the Greenwich Hospital foundation, but the chest itself survives to this day in the National Maritime Museum.

Another event of this period was the painting of the portrait which forms the frontispiece of this book. It was probably done at Drake's London house by Marc Gheerardts about the year 1591. It shows him wearing the jewel presented to him by the Queen after his circumnavigation of the globe. In this sense the jewel, which is preserved at Buckland Abbey, may be regarded as the first naval award.

Drake seems to have been frequently at Court in order to forward his own plans for another cruise to the westward. The idea of capturing Panama attracted him because his old friend John Oxenham had tried and failed to do so with a mere fifty men. Memories of his own successes at Nombre de Dios haunted him during this long period of inactivity. To recall that brilliant exploit to the Queen's mind, he presented her with a manuscript account of the raid, so that rumours were soon flying about that he was going to sea again. 'Sir Francis Drake is at Court, and all the speech is that he goeth very shortly to sea,' wrote a courtier to his brother. Lord Thomas Howard and Sir Martin Frobisher were there too, 'but Sir Francis Drake carryeth it away from them all.'

That was in 1592, but for many reasons the plan was shelved. Philip's intervention in the French Wars of Religion took the form of establishing a Spanish base in Brittany. Two years later Frobisher was killed when Brest was stormed in an unavailing attempt to dislodge the enemy from a position fraught with the greatest danger to the security of the south-western counties of England. Even after Drake's plan had received royal approval that summer, it was postponed again and again because the Queen feared landings on the southern coast. Much to the annoyance of her commanders, she tried to persuade them to search for Spanish forces off Ireland and in the Bay of Biscay before proceeding across the ocean. Drake and Hawkins objected that their force was ill-suited to such a task, but the events of the summer of 1595 proved that the Queen's fears were justified.

On July 23rd four Spanish galleys carrying some 400 soldiers from Brest appeared at Mousehole in Cornwall. The behaviour of the inhabitants was not creditable: they fled inland, leaving Newlyn and other fishing villages to be laid waste in much the same way as Drake had served many a Spanish town. When troops were summoned from the force gathered at Plymouth, most of them deserted on the way. At another landing Penzance was burned, after which the invaders returned unscathed to their base. If this well-timed surprise was not carried out on the same scale as Drake's attack on Cadiz, it was a foretaste of Philip's new offensive policy.

On August 28th, however, after many delays, Drake's expedition was allowed to sail. The reason the Queen changed her mind at such short notice was that news arrived of the wreck off Puerto Rico of the principal treasure ship of that year's fleet. A prize worth two millions seemed to lie waiting for the English. Unfortunately for them, the governor of the island heard at the same time about the fitting out of Drake's expedition. He proceeded to land the treasure in a safe place, fortify the island and summon the ships of the Indian Guard to ensure its defence. The entire lack of secrecy which attended the postponements of Drake's last voyage was one of the principal reasons for its failure.

Another reason was the incomprehensible organization of the command. The armament was composed of twenty-seven sail, of which the Queen provided six, together with 2,500 troops under the command of Sir Thomas Baskerville. For the only time in history two admirals—Drake and Hawkins—shared the command. Each was made responsible for the executive command of his respective squadron, as well as for its victualling and manning. The last time these two sailed together was when Hawkins was in command at

San Juan de Ulua seventeen years previously. Except for the slight coolness between the two cousins after that unhappy affair, there is no evidence that they ever quarrelled, though Drake was never on easy terms with members of the Navy Board over which Hawkins presided. But the two men were of completely different temperaments. Drake's vigorous, impetuous methods were wholly alien to Hawkins's methodical mind. The latter was over sixty years old, a considerable age in those days. On the eve of sailing he heard that his son Richard had been captured at Lima while attempting to repeat Drake's success off South America. He may have wanted to take his revenge, but his slower ways did not make him a congenial companion for his younger cousin, always the brilliant, if rash, opportunist. An infantry captain named Thomas Maynarde, who came to know both of them well on his expedition, describes Hawkins as 'a man old and wary, entering into matters with so leaden a foot that the other's meat would be eaten before his spit could come to the fire: men of so different natures and dispositions that what the one desireth the other would commonly oppose against'.

What persuaded the Queen to divide the command between two such disparate personalities? We have seen how she had of late trusted Hawkins's advice in naval affairs, and she was clear-sighted enough to realize that this venture was a gamble on Drake's part to get himself restored to favour. After the Lisbon failure she had small faith in his administrative abilities. Nor, indeed, does he seem to have learned his lesson in this respect, since there were complaints about bad victualling from the start of this expedition. Maynarde rightly suggests that, as Drake entered upon the venture 'as a child of fortune, it may be his self-willed and peremptory command was doubted.'

The fleet had not been four days at sea before the dissonnance between the temperaments of the two commanders was heard at the councils of war which, on account of the divided command, were held alternatively on board Drake's flagship, the *Defiance*, and on Hawkins's *Garland*. The former complained that he had too many men on board to feed. He asked Hawkins to take some of them off. The latter criticized him for inadequate victualling arrangements. In the end Baskerville had to intervene with a compromise.

Worse was to come. In the Queen's view the capture of the treasure ship at Puerto Rico was the chief aim of the enterprise. For that, speed was essential. Yet Drake insisted that on the way out they should make a landing at the Canary Islands. We can only account for this strange mistake (so out of keeping with his usual practice) on the assumption that he already needed to replenish his food and water. Since Hawkins regarded this as further evidence of bad administration, 'the fire which lay hid in their stomachs began to break forth, and had not the colonel pacified them it would have grown further'.

In the end Hawkins gave in because Baskerville rashly promised to capture the town of Las Palmas in four days. But when they got there, it was obvious that a frontal attack on such a well-fortified place was out of the question. Drake and Baskerville rowed along the coast to find some easier landing place, but no such spot was found because the surf was running high on account of the wind. With difficulty a company of soldiers was put ashore, but they were so badly cut up by the enemy that it became clear that nothing further could be attempted. Meanwhile, for the second time in his career, Drake had narrowly missed a returning treasure fleet composed of thirty ships, which slipped past him to the northward while he was wasting time at the Canaries. Furthermore, an *aviso* (one of Philip's fast sailing vessels which carried the mail to his American colonies) crossed the Atlantic well in advance of the English to warn the governors of the threatened islands of the enemy's approach.

Thus it was that when, at the end of October, Drake and Hawkins reached Guadaloupe the Spanish frigates were ready for them. The *Francis*, a 35-ton bark of Drake's squadron, was cut off as she lagged behind the rest, and taken into Puerto Rico.

It now became apparent how well Drake had succeeded in his Descent on the Indies ten years before. The defence of the islands may have driven Philip nearly bankrupt, but it had now been completed. The chief cities were well fortified and well garrisoned, while ships of the Indian Guard provided a standing naval force such as had been lacking in 1585. At Puerto Rico seventy guns defended the harbour entrance and the fortifications were manned by fifteen hundred regular troops, apart from some nine thousand militia in reserve. A warning shot snapped off the mizen mast of the *Defiance* as she approached, to be followed by another which crashed into Drake's cabin, carrying away the stool on which he was sitting at supper and killing two of his companions. One of them was his particular friend Brute (i.e. Brutus) Brown. Drake's comment on the accident—'Ah, dear Brute, I could grieve for thee, but now is no time for me to let down my spirits'—has been quoted by some biographers as referring to the greater tragedy of Hawkins's death which occurred that same afternoon.

Old Sir John had been suffering from dysentery ever since they reached tropical latitudes. A letter which he wrote to the Queen on his deathbed foretold the failure of the expedition, begging her to recoup her expenses out of his own legacy. It is a pathetic request from a loyal servant of the Crown, who, in spite of much adverse criticism, had laid the foundations of the English fleet just as surely as his family was responsible for the growth of modern Plymouth.

A frontal attack on Puerto Rico being impossible, Drake withdrew his ships out of range in order to search for some other place to land. Since the treasure frigates rode at anchor in a neighbouring bay, he decided to make a night attack with boats to cut them out. At ten o'clock, when it was quite dark (says a Spanish account), twenty-five boats, each carrying fifty well-armed men, pulled in to the attack, though the frigates lay under the protection of shore artillery. The sky was lit by the flashes of a violent bombardment, and by the explosions of grenades ('fire pots') thrown on board the ships by the men in the boats. Fires on board three vessels were soon extinguished, but a fourth burnt so furiously that by the light of the flames the Spanish gunnery became so accurate that after several hours the attack was driven off with the loss of ten boats.

The next day Drake appeared once more in front of the town, but when he saw that the defenders had sunk two blockships in the entrance to the harbour he gave up further attempts and retired to another part of the island to refit his damaged ships. 'I will bring you to twenty places far more wealthy and easier to be gotten,' he assured his companions with desperate optimism. Maynarde, for one, was not convinced: 'Here I left all hope of success,' he notes.

It was decided to seek for better success on the Main itself. After his reception at Puerto Rico, Drake deemed it inadvisable to attack Cartagena (which he had captured so easily ten years ago), but the small town of Rio de la Hacha, at which he had once sold slaves with Hawkins on the voyage of 1568, offered little resistance. However, there was equally little booty to be found, because the inhabitants, after ample warning, had fled to the woods. The governor of a neighbouring pearl fishery offered a ransom of twenty-four thousand *pesos*, which Drake for some reason turned down.

Having burned the place, he proceeded to Nombre de Dios on the isthmus, a town full of heartening memories. Once more the place was taken, but once more the inhabitants had received ample warning of his approach. This time Baskerville with seven hundred and fifty picked men went inland in search of them along the very same road on which Drake had once ambushed the mule trains from Panama. This time it was the Englishmen's turn to be ambushed in a narrow defile in pouring rain. The remnant of the force retreated, wet, hungry and shoeless, to the refuge of their ships. Maynarde, who was one of the few survivors, describes them as 'so wearied with the illness of the way, surbaited (i.e. bruised) for want of shoes, and weak with their diet that it would have been a poor day's service that we should have done upon an enemy had they been there to resist us'.

This was on 2nd January, 1596. For the first time Drake admitted failure: 'Since our return from Panama he never carried mirth nor joy in his face.' Twenty bars of silver and two quoits of gold were all that he had to show for the capture of the town which was once known as the treasure house of the world. But he was still enough of a leader to try to keep up the spirits of his men. 'It matters not, man,' he told Maynarde, 'God hath many things in store for us; and I know many means to do Her Majesty good service and to make us rich, for we must have gold before we see England.'

Where was gold to be found? There was little prospect of anything to the northward, though the Spaniards were building a new town further up the coast which was to be called Porto Bello. It was the unhealthiest place in the West Indies, but it was the only chance of recouping their fortunes before they returned to what, for Drake, would have been an ignominious eclipse from public life. As the fleet stood northward fever and dysentery increased among the disillusioned men on board, and for almost the first time in his life Drake himself fell ill.

By the time the *Defiance* anchored under the lee of the island of Escuedo de Veragua, thirty leagues from Porto Bello, he was a dying man. In his delirium he raved against traitors. Rising from his bed, he started to put his armour on, declaring that he would meet death like a soldier. Then he fell back exhausted. 'Yielding up his spirit like a Christian to his Creator' he died quietly in his cabin an hour later at seven o'clock on the morning of 28th January, 1596.

The next day Baskerville, who succeeded to the command after the death of the two admirals, carried his body a league out to sea, where he received a sailor's burial.

The expedition was brought home a few weeks later, having accomplished nothing. But that summer the brilliant capture of Cadiz by the flower of Elizabethan chivalry—Essex, Raleigh, Lord Thomas Howard and his cousin the Lord Admiral himself—atoned for the failure of the last big expedition to the West Indies before the capture of Jamaica and the establishment of the first English colony in those parts sixty-five years later.

For centuries to come memories of Drake's earlier successes remained fresh in the minds of the inhabitants of those parts. The hardy buccaneers of a hundred years later (Drake's true disciples) constantly appealed to his example when they renewed English attacks on Spanish possessions. When Sir Edward Vernon captured Porto Bello in the eighteenth century, it was felt by many that Drake's death had been avenged. A verse from an innocent piece of doggerel by an obscure poet named Robert Hayman (who became the governor of Newfoundland) gives a more intimate and charming picture of how the Drake tradition was handed down by small boys in his native Devonshire. The poem is entitled *Of the great and famous ever to be honoured knight Sir Francis and of my little little self.*

> *This man when little I did meet*
> *As he was walking up Totnes long street.*
> *He asked me who I was? I answered him.*
> *He asked me if his good friend was within?*
> *A fair red orange in his hand he had.*
> *He gave it me, whereof I was right glad,*
> *Takes and kissed me, and prays 'God bless my boy',*
> *Which I record with comfort to this day.*

An anonymous writer of that generation has left us Drake's true epitaph:

> *The waves became his winding sheet; the waters were his tomb;*
> *But for his fame the ocean sea was not sufficient room.*

A Selected List of Books

The standard biography of Drake is Sir Julian Corbett's *Drake and The Tudor Navy* (1898). Good general surveys of the background of his life will be found in J. A. Williamson's *Age of Drake* (1938) and A. L. Rowse's *The Expansion of England* (1955).

The original narratives and documents, apart from those printed in Hakluyt's *Principal Navigations* (Everyman Library,) 8 vols., will be found in three volumes edited for the Hakluyt Society by Irene Wright—*Spanish Documents concerning English Voyages to the Caribbean, 1527–68* (1928); ditto *1568–80* (1932); *Further English Voyages 1583–94* (1951). These may be supplemented by other volumes issued by the same Society—*The Roanoke Voyages* (ed. Quinn, 1955); *New Light on Drake* (ed. Nuttall, 1974); *The Last Voyage of Drake and Hawkins* (ed. Andrews, 1972). A useful collection of the narratives of his voyages, including that round the world, will be found in *Francis Drake Privateer*, ed. J. Hampden (1972) and an up-to-date commentary on his career is *Drake's Voyages* by K. R. Andrews (1967).

For the voyage round the world, see Sir Richard Temple's edition of *The World Encompassed* (Argonaut Press, 1926) and H. R. Wagner's *Sir Francis Drake's Voyage Round the World* (Californian Historical Society, 1926). The catalogue by Helen Wallis of the exhibition celebrating the fourth centenary of the voyage at the British Library contains the most recent information.

For the Spanish War, see the volumes published by the Navy Records Society—*Monson's Tracts* (ed. M. Oppenheim, 1902); *Papers Relating to the Defeat of the Spanish Armada* (ed. J. K. Laughton, 1895); *Papers Relating to the Spanish War* (ed. J. Corbett, 1898); *Naval Miscellany, Vol IV* (ed. C. Lloyd, 1952) for Ubaldino's second narrative (ed G.P. Naish). The best account is Garrett Mattingly's The *Defeat of the Spanish Armada* (1959). For underwater archaeology, see R. Stenuit's *Treasure of the Armada* (1972).

Many valuable incidental articles on Drake have appeared in *The Mariner's Mirror*, especially vols. 15, 16, 35, 37, 39 and 64.

For the history of the family, see Lady Eliott Drake's *Heirs and Successors of Sir Francis Drake*.

Index